WORDLE TUMBLE

200 wordle chains to do anywhere, anytime

How to use this book

In **Wordle Tumble**, you use letter prompts to find a five-letter word suggested by the clue. The letters in this word give you further prompts to find the next solution, and so on...

The appearance of each letter tells you **if** it occurs in the solution and **where** it appears.

A white letter on a black background means that the letter is in the solution and in the correct position, for example the letters **S** and **H** below:

S H I L L

A black letter on a grey background shows that the letter is in the solution but in the wrong position, for example the letters **H**, **O** and **S** below:

H O U S E

A black letter on a white background means that the letter is not in the solution at all, for example the letters **B**, **R** and **A** below:

B R A V E

The clue is **PUSH** so the solution is **SHOVE**.

S H O V E

The appearance of the solution boxes gives prompts to find the next solution.

A white box with a black border means that the letter appears in the following solution in the same position, in this case **H** and **E**.

A grey box means that the letter appears in the following solution, but in a different position, in this case **S**.

A blank white box means that the letter does not appear in the following solution at all, in this case **O** and **V**.

Using the subsequent prompts and the clue **HUNT**, we can find the next solution:

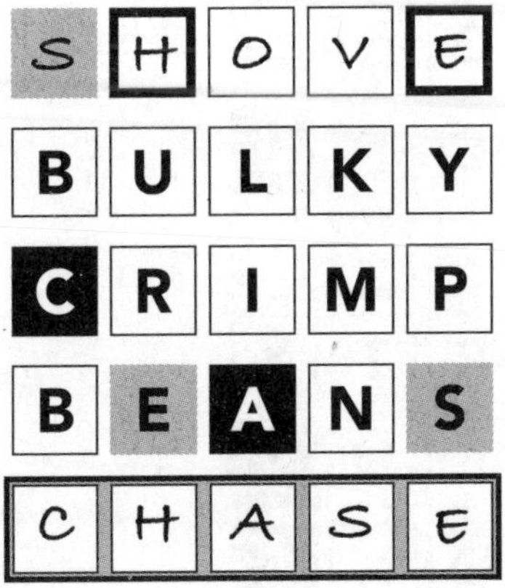

For each clue there is a letter marker, so you can keep track of which letters have been ruled out, like this:

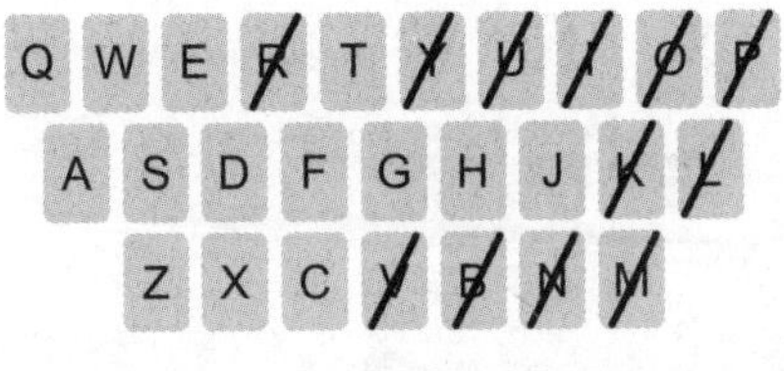

The **EASY** puzzles contain more correct letters, more frequently in their correct positions. The **MEDIUM** puzzles give you fewer correct letters. The **EXPERT** puzzles are twice as long.

Good luck!

Puzzle 1

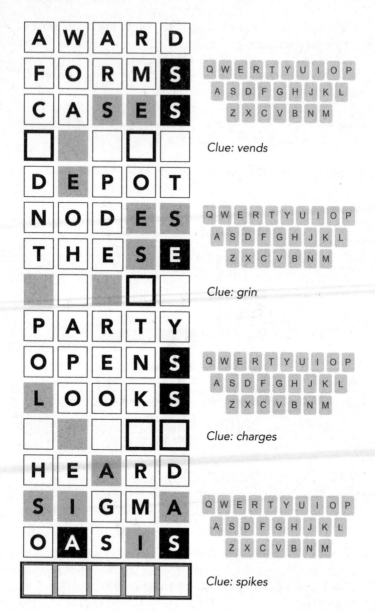

A	W	A	R	D
F	O	R	M	S
C	A	S	E	S
D	E	P	O	T
N	O	D	E	S
T	H	E	S	E
P	A	R	T	Y
O	P	E	N	S
L	O	O	K	S
H	E	A	R	D
S	I	G	M	A
O	A	S	I	S

Q W E R T Y U I O P
A S D F G H J K L
Z X C V B N M

Clue: vends

Q W E R T Y U I O P
A S D F G H J K L
Z X C V B N M

Clue: grin

Q W E R T Y U I O P
A S D F G H J K L
Z X C V B N M

Clue: charges

Q W E R T Y U I O P
A S D F G H J K L
Z X C V B N M

Clue: spikes

Puzzle 2

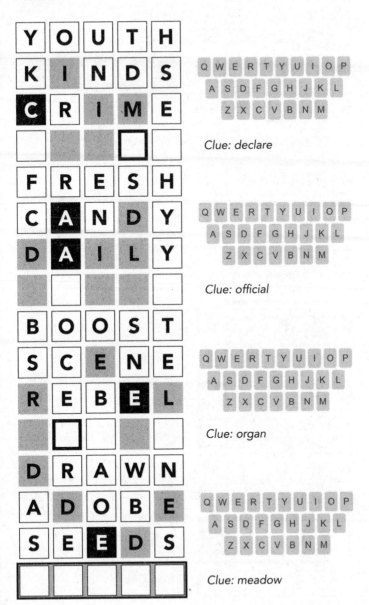

Y	O	U	T	H
K	I	N	D	S
C	R	I	M	E

Q W E R T Y U I O P
A S D F G H J K L
Z X C V B N M

Clue: declare

F	R	E	S	H
C	A	N	D	Y
D	A	I	L	Y

Q W E R T Y U I O P
A S D F G H J K L
Z X C V B N M

Clue: official

B	O	O	S	T
S	C	E	N	E
R	E	B	E	L

Q W E R T Y U I O P
A S D F G H J K L
Z X C V B N M

Clue: organ

D	R	A	W	N
A	D	O	B	E
S	E	E	D	S

Q W E R T Y U I O P
A S D F G H J K L
Z X C V B N M

Clue: meadow

Puzzle 3

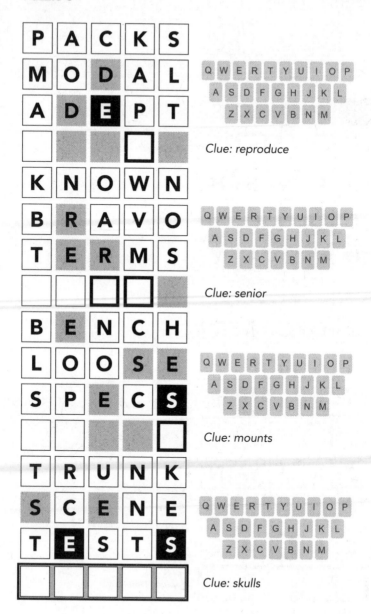

P	A	C	K	S
M	O	D	A	L
A	D	E	P	T
K	N	O	W	N
B	R	A	V	O
T	E	R	M	S
B	E	N	C	H
L	O	O	S	E
S	P	E	C	S
T	R	U	N	K
S	C	E	N	E
T	E	S	T	S

Q W E R T Y U I O P
A S D F G H J K L
Z X C V B N M

Clue: reproduce

Q W E R T Y U I O P
A S D F G H J K L
Z X C V B N M

Clue: senior

Q W E R T Y U I O P
A S D F G H J K L
Z X C V B N M

Clue: mounts

Q W E R T Y U I O P
A S D F G H J K L
Z X C V B N M

Clue: skulls

Puzzle 4

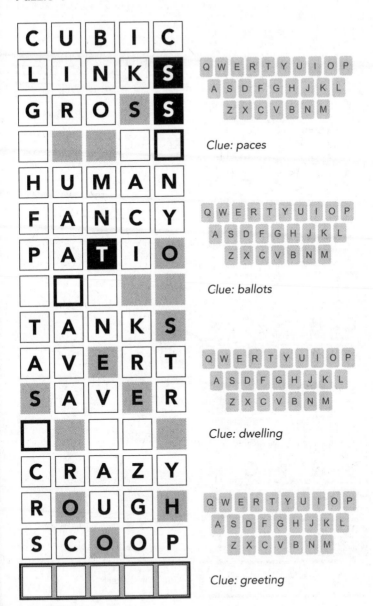

C	U	B	I	C
L	I	N	K	S
G	R	O	S	S
H	U	M	A	N
F	A	N	C	Y
P	A	T	I	O
T	A	N	K	S
A	V	E	R	T
S	A	V	E	R
C	R	A	Z	Y
R	O	U	G	H
S	C	O	O	P

Q W E R T Y U I O P
A S D F G H J K L
Z X C V B N M

Clue: paces

Q W E R T Y U I O P
A S D F G H J K L
Z X C V B N M

Clue: ballots

Q W E R T Y U I O P
A S D F G H J K L
Z X C V B N M

Clue: dwelling

Q W E R T Y U I O P
A S D F G H J K L
Z X C V B N M

Clue: greeting

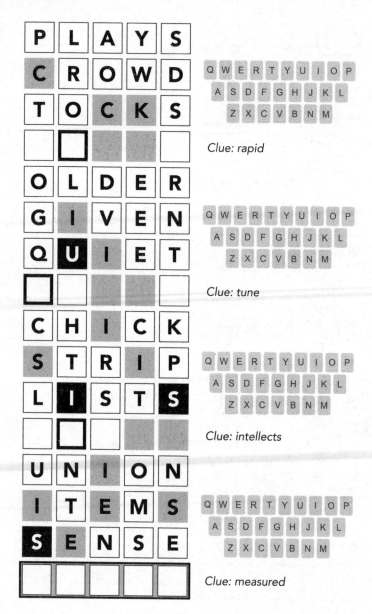

Puzzle 5

P	L	A	Y	S
C	R	O	W	D
T	O	C	K	S
O	L	D	E	R
G	I	V	E	N
Q	U	I	E	T
C	H	I	C	K
S	T	R	I	P
L	I	S	T	S
U	N	I	O	N
I	T	E	M	S
S	E	N	S	E

Q W E R T Y U I O P
A S D F G H J K L
Z X C V B N M

Clue: rapid

Q W E R T Y U I O P
A S D F G H J K L
Z X C V B N M

Clue: tune

Q W E R T Y U I O P
A S D F G H J K L
Z X C V B N M

Clue: intellects

Q W E R T Y U I O P
A S D F G H J K L
Z X C V B N M

Clue: measured

Puzzle 6

C	O	U	L	D
R	E	S	A	Y
D	R	A	W	N

Q W E R T Y U I O P
A S D F G H J K L
Z X C V B N M

Clue: fish

A	P	P	L	E
L	E	A	S	T
S	A	N	T	A

Q W E R T Y U I O P
A S D F G H J K L
Z X C V B N M

Clue: sweet

M	I	X	E	R
A	R	G	U	E
L	U	N	A	R

Q W E R T Y U I O P
A S D F G H J K L
Z X C V B N M

Clue: sears

A	L	L	O	Y
G	A	U	G	E
Q	U	E	U	E

Q W E R T Y U I O P
A S D F G H J K L
Z X C V B N M

Clue: liquid

Puzzle 7

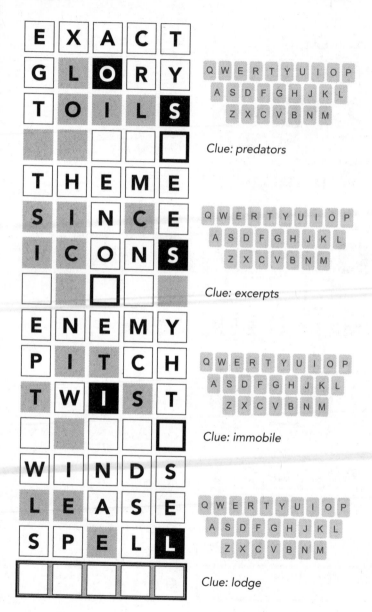

E	X	A	C	T
G	L	O	R	Y
T	O	I	L	S
T	H	E	M	E
S	I	N	C	E
I	C	O	N	S
E	N	E	M	Y
P	I	T	C	H
T	W	I	S	T
W	I	N	D	S
L	E	A	S	E
S	P	E	L	L

Q W E R T Y U I O P
A S D F G H J K L
Z X C V B N M

Clue: predators

Q W E R T Y U I O P
A S D F G H J K L
Z X C V B N M

Clue: excerpts

Q W E R T Y U I O P
A S D F G H J K L
Z X C V B N M

Clue: immobile

Q W E R T Y U I O P
A S D F G H J K L
Z X C V B N M

Clue: lodge

Puzzle 8

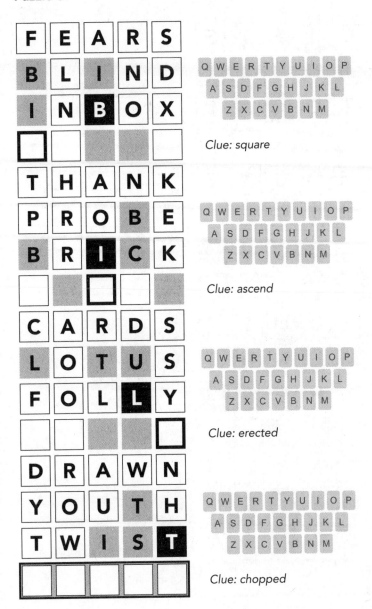

F	E	A	R	S
B	L	I	N	D
I	N	B	O	X

Q W E R T Y U I O P
A S D F G H J K L
Z X C V B N M

Clue: square

T	H	A	N	K
P	R	O	B	E
B	R	I	C	K

Q W E R T Y U I O P
A S D F G H J K L
Z X C V B N M

Clue: ascend

C	A	R	D	S
L	O	T	U	S
F	O	L	L	Y

Q W E R T Y U I O P
A S D F G H J K L
Z X C V B N M

Clue: erected

D	R	A	W	N
Y	O	U	T	H
T	W	I	S	T

Q W E R T Y U I O P
A S D F G H J K L
Z X C V B N M

Clue: chopped

EASY

Puzzle 9

G	I	F	T	S
A	D	U	L	T
T	O	T	A	L

Q W E R T Y U I O P
A S D F G H J K L
Z X C V B N M

Clue: mend

M	O	U	N	T
T	I	G	H	T
A	B	O	V	E

Q W E R T Y U I O P
A S D F G H J K L
Z X C V B N M

Clue: expanse

A	U	D	I	T
M	E	N	U	S
T	H	E	S	E

Q W E R T Y U I O P
A S D F G H J K L
Z X C V B N M

Clue: range

T	A	K	E	N
M	E	R	C	Y
S	C	R	E	W

Q W E R T Y U I O P
A S D F G H J K L
Z X C V B N M

Clue: unit

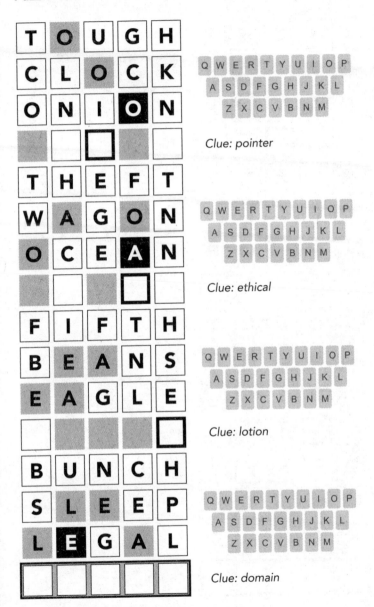

Puzzle 10

T	O	U	G	H
C	L	O	C	K
O	N	I	O	N
T	H	E	F	T
W	A	G	O	N
O	C	E	A	N
F	I	F	T	H
B	E	A	N	S
E	A	G	L	E
B	U	N	C	H
S	L	E	E	P
L	E	G	A	L

Q W E R T Y U I O P
A S D F G H J K L
Z X C V B N M

Clue: pointer

Q W E R T Y U I O P
A S D F G H J K L
Z X C V B N M

Clue: ethical

Q W E R T Y U I O P
A S D F G H J K L
Z X C V B N M

Clue: lotion

Q W E R T Y U I O P
A S D F G H J K L
Z X C V B N M

Clue: domain

EASY

Puzzle 11

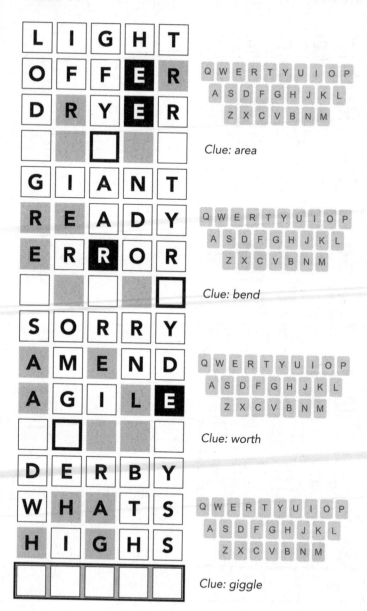

L	I	G	H	T
O	F	F	E	R
D	R	Y	E	R
G	I	A	N	T
R	E	A	D	Y
E	R	R	O	R
S	O	R	R	Y
A	M	E	N	D
A	G	I	L	E
D	E	R	B	Y
W	H	A	T	S
H	I	G	H	S

Q W E R T Y U I O P
A S D F G H J K L
Z X C V B N M

Clue: area

Q W E R T Y U I O P
A S D F G H J K L
Z X C V B N M

Clue: bend

Q W E R T Y U I O P
A S D F G H J K L
Z X C V B N M

Clue: worth

Q W E R T Y U I O P
A S D F G H J K L
Z X C V B N M

Clue: giggle

Puzzle 12

F	I	F	T	H
O	R	D	E	R
P	R	O	P	S
E	X	T	R	A
B	E	A	C	H
S	H	E	E	R
B	R	I	D	E
D	E	P	O	T
A	D	D	E	D
W	H	I	L	E
S	T	R	I	P
R	O	C	K	S

Q W E R T Y U I O P
A S D F G H J K L
Z X C V B N M

Clue: dispatches

Q W E R T Y U I O P
A S D F G H J K L
Z X C V B N M

Clue: areas

Q W E R T Y U I O P
A S D F G H J K L
Z X C V B N M

Clue: noise

Q W E R T Y U I O P
A S D F G H J K L
Z X C V B N M

Clue: rotates

Puzzle 13

L	O	D	G	E
S	A	T	I	N
U	S	E	R	S

Q W E R T Y U I O P
A S D F G H J K L
Z X C V B N M

Clue: dollars

D	R	A	F	T
T	Y	P	E	S
L	I	V	E	S

Q W E R T Y U I O P
A S D F G H J K L
Z X C V B N M

Clue: groups

T	H	I	R	D
C	A	M	E	L
B	L	A	M	E

Q W E R T Y U I O P
A S D F G H J K L
Z X C V B N M

Clue: record

O	W	N	E	R
D	A	I	R	Y
A	L	O	U	D

Q W E R T Y U I O P
A S D F G H J K L
Z X C V B N M

Clue: mature

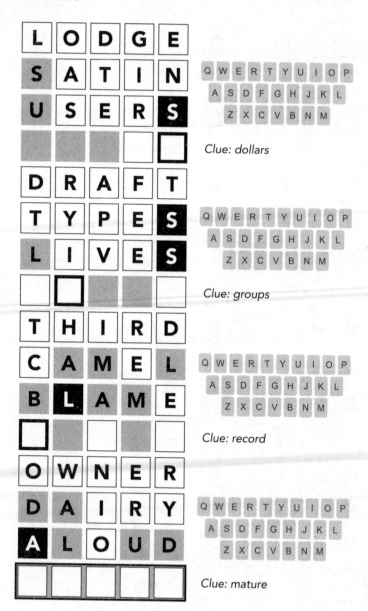

Puzzle 14

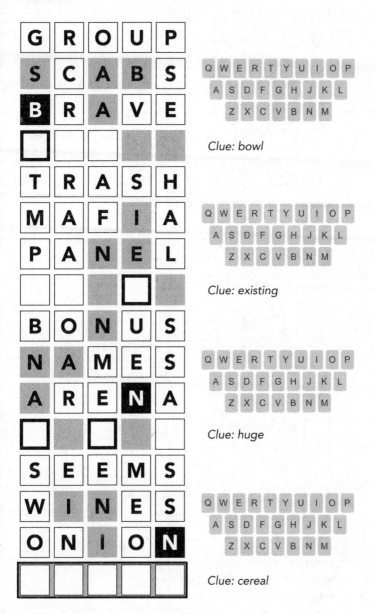

G	R	O	U	P
S	C	A	B	S
B	R	A	V	E

Q W E R T Y U I O P
A S D F G H J K L
Z X C V B N M

Clue: bowl

T	R	A	S	H
M	A	F	I	A
P	A	N	E	L

Q W E R T Y U I O P
A S D F G H J K L
Z X C V B N M

Clue: existing

B	O	N	U	S
N	A	M	E	S
A	R	E	N	A

Q W E R T Y U I O P
A S D F G H J K L
Z X C V B N M

Clue: huge

S	E	E	M	S
W	I	N	E	S
O	N	I	O	N

Q W E R T Y U I O P
A S D F G H J K L
Z X C V B N M

Clue: cereal

Puzzle 15

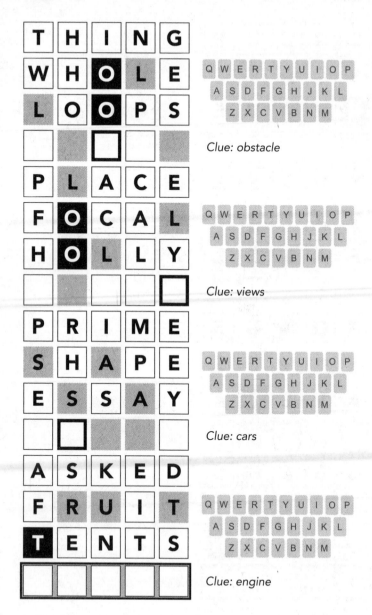

T	H	I	N	G
W	H	O	L	E
L	O	O	P	S
P	L	A	C	E
F	O	C	A	L
H	O	L	L	Y
P	R	I	M	E
S	H	A	P	E
E	S	S	A	Y
A	S	K	E	D
F	R	U	I	T
T	E	N	T	S

Q W E R T Y U I O P
A S D F G H J K L
Z X C V B N M

Clue: obstacle

Q W E R T Y U I O P
A S D F G H J K L
Z X C V B N M

Clue: views

Q W E R T Y U I O P
A S D F G H J K L
Z X C V B N M

Clue: cars

Q W E R T Y U I O P
A S D F G H J K L
Z X C V B N M

Clue: engine

Puzzle 16

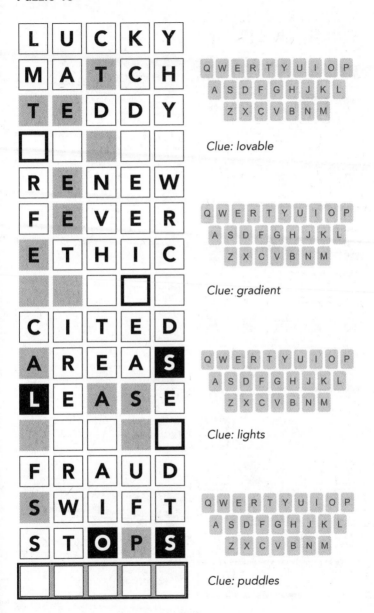

L	U	C	K	Y
M	A	T	C	H
T	E	D	D	Y
R	E	N	E	W
F	E	V	E	R
E	T	H	I	C
C	I	T	E	D
A	R	E	A	S
L	E	A	S	E
F	R	A	U	D
S	W	I	F	T
S	T	O	P	S

Q W E R T Y U I O P
A S D F G H J K L
Z X C V B N M

Clue: lovable

Q W E R T Y U I O P
A S D F G H J K L
Z X C V B N M

Clue: gradient

Q W E R T Y U I O P
A S D F G H J K L
Z X C V B N M

Clue: lights

Q W E R T Y U I O P
A S D F G H J K L
Z X C V B N M

Clue: puddles

Puzzle 17

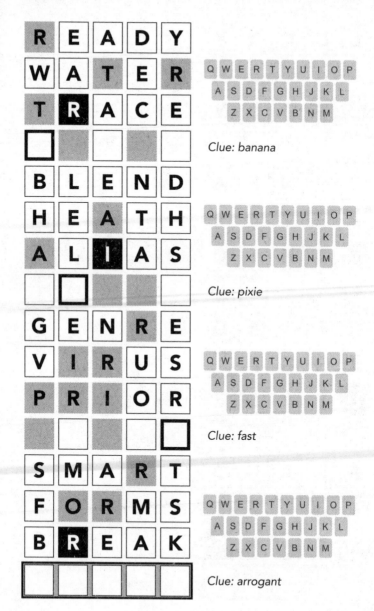

R	E	A	D	Y
W	A	T	E	R
T	R	A	C	E

Q W E R T Y U I O P
A S D F G H J K L
Z X C V B N M

Clue: banana

B	L	E	N	D
H	E	A	T	H
A	L	I	A	S

Q W E R T Y U I O P
A S D F G H J K L
Z X C V B N M

Clue: pixie

G	E	N	R	E
V	I	R	U	S
P	R	I	O	R

Q W E R T Y U I O P
A S D F G H J K L
Z X C V B N M

Clue: fast

S	M	A	R	T
F	O	R	M	S
B	R	E	A	K

Q W E R T Y U I O P
A S D F G H J K L
Z X C V B N M

Clue: arrogant

Puzzle 18

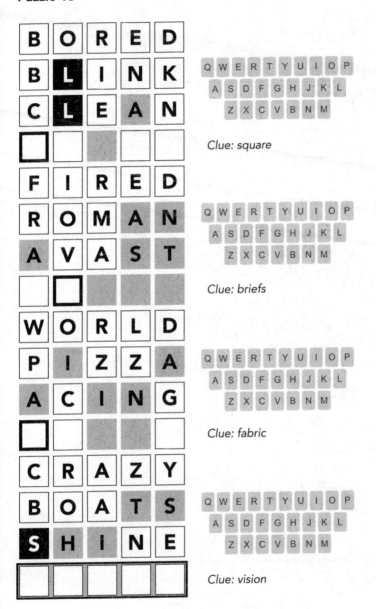

B	O	R	E	D
B	L	I	N	K
C	L	E	A	N
F	I	R	E	D
R	O	M	A	N
A	V	A	S	T
W	O	R	L	D
P	I	Z	Z	A
A	C	I	N	G
C	R	A	Z	Y
B	O	A	T	S
S	H	I	N	E

Q W E R T Y U I O P
A S D F G H J K L
Z X C V B N M

Clue: square

Q W E R T Y U I O P
A S D F G H J K L
Z X C V B N M

Clue: briefs

Q W E R T Y U I O P
A S D F G H J K L
Z X C V B N M

Clue: fabric

Q W E R T Y U I O P
A S D F G H J K L
Z X C V B N M

Clue: vision

EASY

Puzzle 19

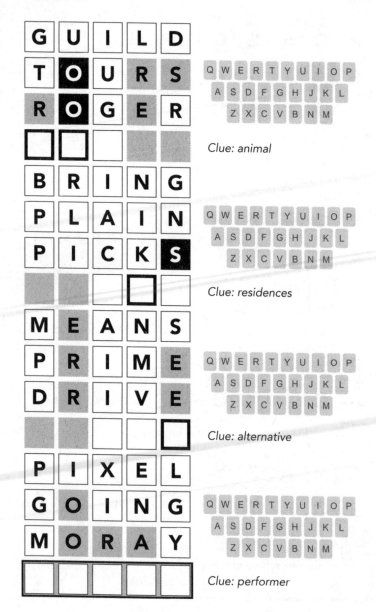

G	U	I	L	D	
T	O	U	R	S	Q W E R T Y U I O P
R	O	G	E	R	A S D F G H J K L Z X C V B N M
					Clue: animal
B	R	I	N	G	
P	L	A	I	N	Q W E R T Y U I O P
P	I	C	K	S	A S D F G H J K L Z X C V B N M
					Clue: residences
M	E	A	N	S	
P	R	I	M	E	Q W E R T Y U I O P
D	R	I	V	E	A S D F G H J K L Z X C V B N M
					Clue: alternative
P	I	X	E	L	
G	O	I	N	G	Q W E R T Y U I O P
M	O	R	A	Y	A S D F G H J K L Z X C V B N M
					Clue: performer

Puzzle 20

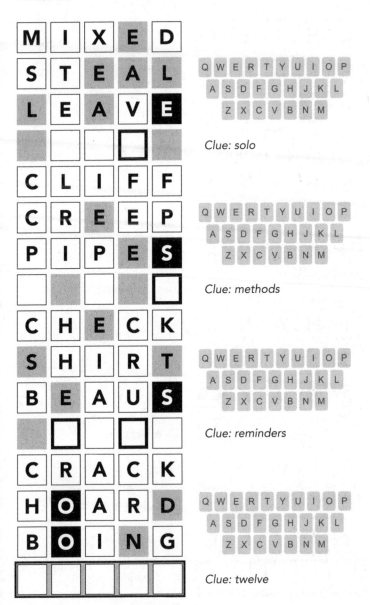

M	I	X	E	D
S	T	E	A	L
L	E	A	V	E

Q W E R T Y U I O P
A S D F G H J K L
Z X C V B N M

Clue: solo

C	L	I	F	F
C	R	E	E	P
P	I	P	E	S

Q W E R T Y U I O P
A S D F G H J K L
Z X C V B N M

Clue: methods

C	H	E	C	K
S	H	I	R	T
B	E	A	U	S

Q W E R T Y U I O P
A S D F G H J K L
Z X C V B N M

Clue: reminders

C	R	A	C	K
H	O	A	R	D
B	O	I	N	G

Q W E R T Y U I O P
A S D F G H J K L
Z X C V B N M

Clue: twelve

Puzzle 21

C	H	I	E	F
B	L	A	N	D
L	A	K	E	S
B	U	N	N	Y
W	I	R	E	D
D	R	I	V	E
T	H	A	N	K
O	L	D	E	R
L	E	A	K	S
B	L	O	O	D
A	G	O	N	Y
T	I	T	L	E

Q W E R T Y U I O P
A S D F G H J K L
Z X C V B N M

Clue: father

Q W E R T Y U I O P
A S D F G H J K L
Z X C V B N M

Clue: communication

Q W E R T Y U I O P
A S D F G H J K L
Z X C V B N M

Clue: distance

Q W E R T Y U I O P
A S D F G H J K L
Z X C V B N M

Clue: parts

EASY

Puzzle 22

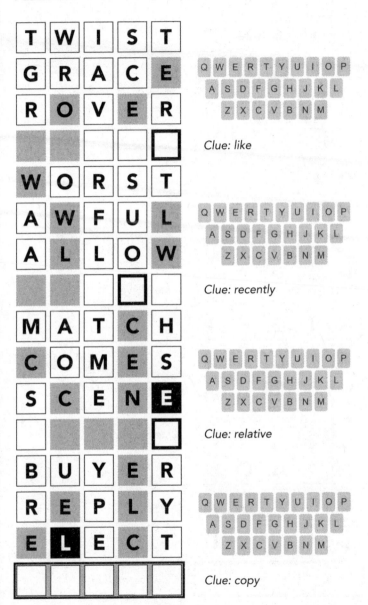

T	W	I	S	T
G	R	A	C	E
R	O	V	E	R
W	O	R	S	T
A	W	F	U	L
A	L	L	O	W
M	A	T	C	H
C	O	M	E	S
S	C	E	N	E
B	U	Y	E	R
R	E	P	L	Y
E	L	E	C	T

Q W E R T Y U I O P
A S D F G H J K L
Z X C V B N M

Clue: like

Q W E R T Y U I O P
A S D F G H J K L
Z X C V B N M

Clue: recently

Q W E R T Y U I O P
A S D F G H J K L
Z X C V B N M

Clue: relative

Q W E R T Y U I O P
A S D F G H J K L
Z X C V B N M

Clue: copy

EASY

Puzzle 23

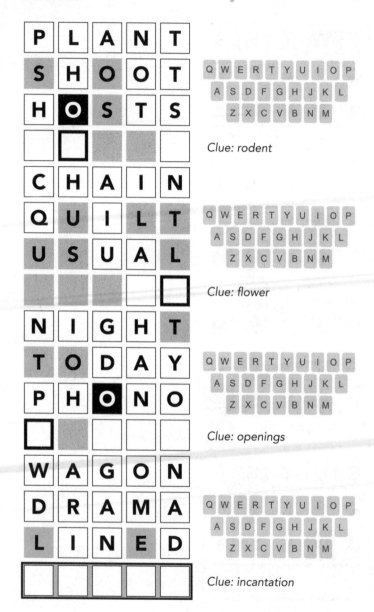

P	L	A	N	T
S	H	O	O	T
H	O	S	T	S

Q W E R T Y U I O P
A S D F G H J K L
Z X C V B N M

Clue: rodent

C	H	A	I	N
Q	U	I	L	T
U	S	U	A	L

Q W E R T Y U I O P
A S D F G H J K L
Z X C V B N M

Clue: flower

N	I	G	H	T
T	O	D	A	Y
P	H	O	N	O

Q W E R T Y U I O P
A S D F G H J K L
Z X C V B N M

Clue: openings

W	A	G	O	N
D	R	A	M	A
L	I	N	E	D

Q W E R T Y U I O P
A S D F G H J K L
Z X C V B N M

Clue: incantation

EASY

Puzzle 24

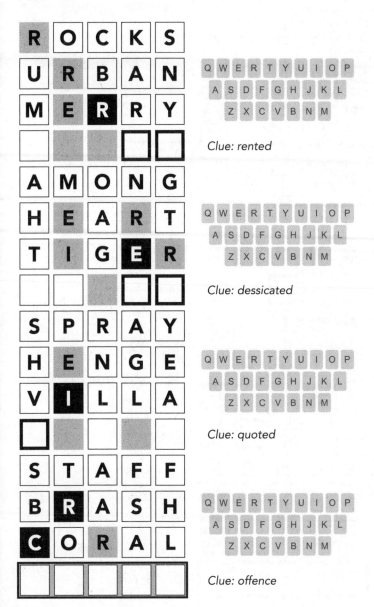

R	O	C	K	S
U	R	B	A	N
M	E	R	R	Y
A	M	O	N	G
H	E	A	R	T
T	I	G	E	R
S	P	R	A	Y
H	E	N	G	E
V	I	L	L	A
S	T	A	F	F
B	R	A	S	H
C	O	R	A	L

Q W E R T Y U I O P
A S D F G H J K L
Z X C V B N M

Clue: rented

Q W E R T Y U I O P
A S D F G H J K L
Z X C V B N M

Clue: dessicated

Q W E R T Y U I O P
A S D F G H J K L
Z X C V B N M

Clue: quoted

Q W E R T Y U I O P
A S D F G H J K L
Z X C V B N M

Clue: offence

E A S Y

Puzzle 25

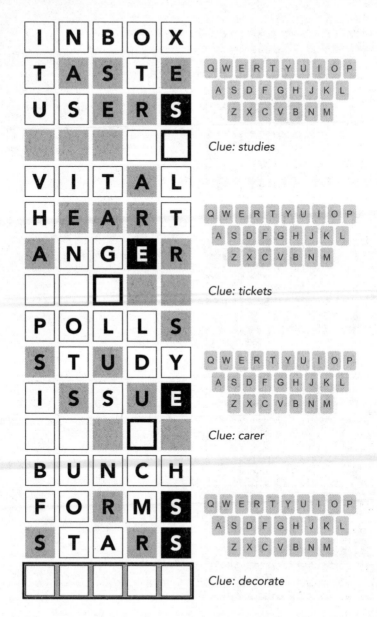

I	N	B	O	X	
T	A	S	T	E	Q W E R T Y U I O P / A S D F G H J K L / Z X C V B N M
U	S	E	R	S	
					Clue: studies
V	I	T	A	L	
H	E	A	R	T	Q W E R T Y U I O P / A S D F G H J K L / Z X C V B N M
A	N	G	E	R	
					Clue: tickets
P	O	L	L	S	
S	T	U	D	Y	Q W E R T Y U I O P / A S D F G H J K L / Z X C V B N M
I	S	S	U	E	
					Clue: carer
B	U	N	C	H	
F	O	R	M	S	Q W E R T Y U I O P / A S D F G H J K L / Z X C V B N M
S	T	A	R	S	
					Clue: decorate

EASY

Puzzle 26

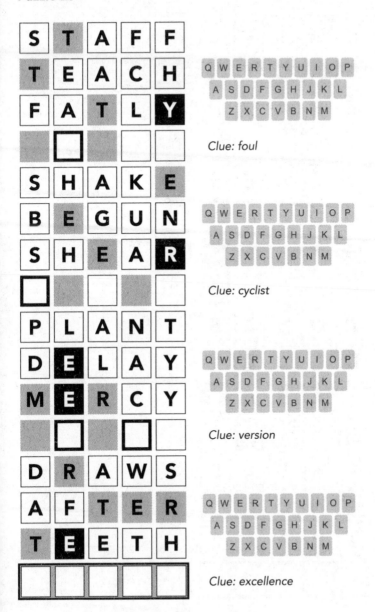

S	T	A	F	F
T	E	A	C	H
F	A	T	L	Y

Q W E R T Y U I O P
A S D F G H J K L
Z X C V B N M

Clue: foul

S	H	A	K	E
B	E	G	U	N
S	H	E	A	R

Q W E R T Y U I O P
A S D F G H J K L
Z X C V B N M

Clue: cyclist

P	L	A	N	T
D	E	L	A	Y
M	E	R	C	Y

Q W E R T Y U I O P
A S D F G H J K L
Z X C V B N M

Clue: version

D	R	A	W	S
A	F	T	E	R
T	E	E	T	H

Q W E R T Y U I O P
A S D F G H J K L
Z X C V B N M

Clue: excellence

E
A
S
Y

Puzzle 27

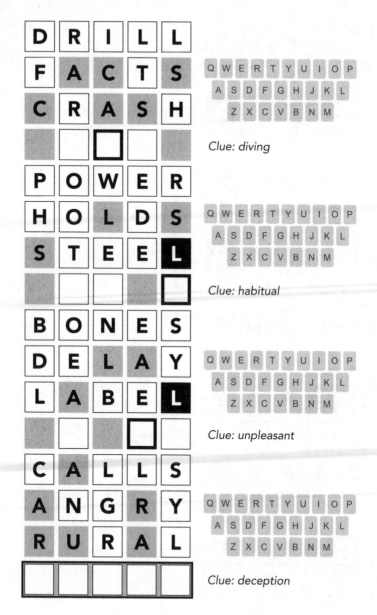

D	R	I	L	L
F	A	C	T	S
C	R	A	S	H

Q W E R T Y U I O P
A S D F G H J K L
Z X C V B N M

Clue: diving

P	O	W	E	R
H	O	L	D	S
S	T	E	E	L

Q W E R T Y U I O P
A S D F G H J K L
Z X C V B N M

Clue: habitual

B	O	N	E	S
D	E	L	A	Y
L	A	B	E	L

Q W E R T Y U I O P
A S D F G H J K L
Z X C V B N M

Clue: unpleasant

C	A	L	L	S
A	N	G	R	Y
R	U	R	A	L

Q W E R T Y U I O P
A S D F G H J K L
Z X C V B N M

Clue: deception

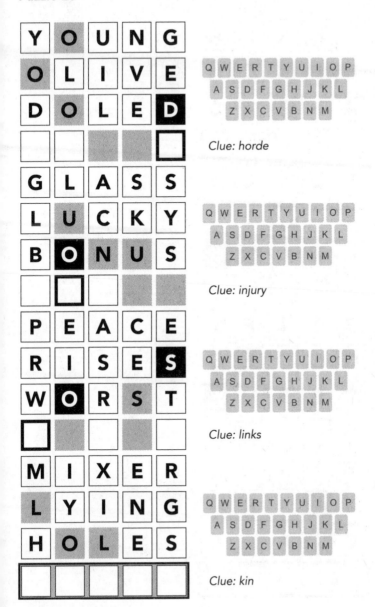

Puzzle 28

Y	O	U	N	G
O	L	I	V	E
D	O	L	E	D
G	L	A	S	S
L	U	C	K	Y
B	O	N	U	S
P	E	A	C	E
R	I	S	E	S
W	O	R	S	T
M	I	X	E	R
L	Y	I	N	G
H	O	L	E	S

Q W E R T Y U I O P
A S D F G H J K L
Z X C V B N M

Clue: horde

Q W E R T Y U I O P
A S D F G H J K L
Z X C V B N M

Clue: injury

Q W E R T Y U I O P
A S D F G H J K L
Z X C V B N M

Clue: links

Q W E R T Y U I O P
A S D F G H J K L
Z X C V B N M

Clue: kin

Puzzle 29

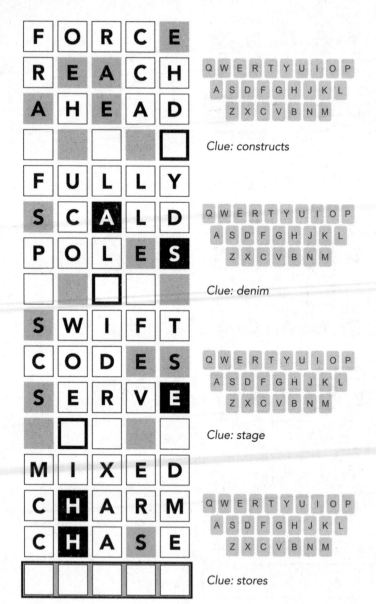

F	O	R	C	E
R	E	A	C	H
A	H	E	A	D

QWERTYUIOP
ASDFGHJKL
ZXCVBNM

Clue: constructs

F	U	L	L	Y
S	C	A	L	D
P	O	L	E	S

QWERTYUIOP
ASDFGHJKL
ZXCVBNM

Clue: denim

S	W	I	F	T
C	O	D	E	S
S	E	R	V	E

QWERTYUIOP
ASDFGHJKL
ZXCVBNM

Clue: stage

M	I	X	E	D
C	H	A	R	M
C	H	A	S	E

QWERTYUIOP
ASDFGHJKL
ZXCVBNM

Clue: stores

Puzzle 30

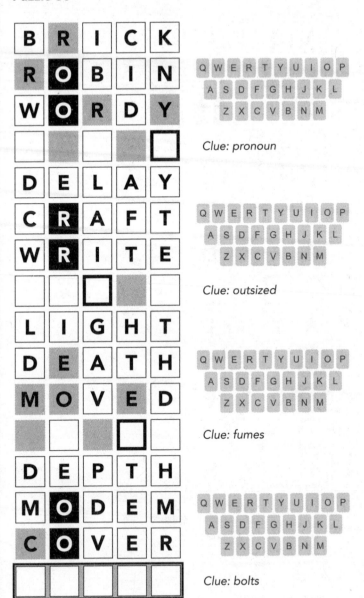

B	R	I	C	K
R	O	B	I	N
W	O	R	D	Y
D	E	L	A	Y
C	R	A	F	T
W	R	I	T	E
L	I	G	H	T
D	E	A	T	H
M	O	V	E	D
D	E	P	T	H
M	O	D	E	M
C	O	V	E	R

Q W E R T Y U I O P
A S D F G H J K L
Z X C V B N M

Clue: pronoun

Q W E R T Y U I O P
A S D F G H J K L
Z X C V B N M

Clue: outsized

Q W E R T Y U I O P
A S D F G H J K L
Z X C V B N M

Clue: fumes

Q W E R T Y U I O P
A S D F G H J K L
Z X C V B N M

Clue: bolts

E
A
S
Y

Puzzle 31

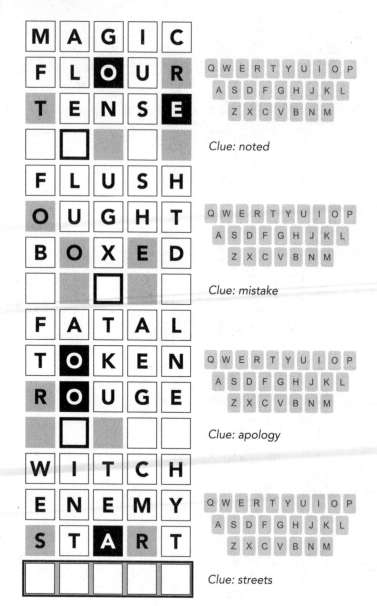

M	A	G	I	C
F	L	O	U	R
T	E	N	S	E

Q W E R T Y U I O P
A S D F G H J K L
Z X C V B N M

Clue: noted

F	L	U	S	H
O	U	G	H	T
B	O	X	E	D

Q W E R T Y U I O P
A S D F G H J K L
Z X C V B N M

Clue: mistake

F	A	T	A	L
T	O	K	E	N
R	O	U	G	E

Q W E R T Y U I O P
A S D F G H J K L
Z X C V B N M

Clue: apology

W	I	T	C	H
E	N	E	M	Y
S	T	A	R	T

Q W E R T Y U I O P
A S D F G H J K L
Z X C V B N M

Clue: streets

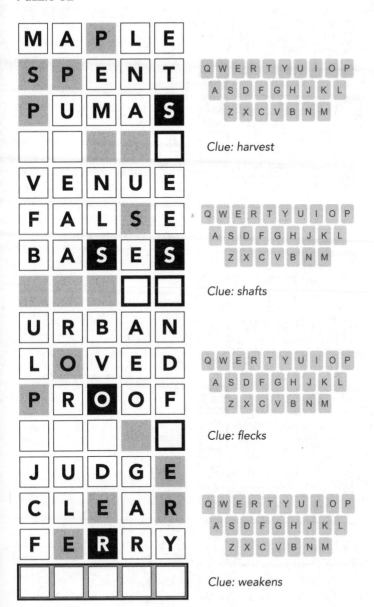

Puzzle 32

M	A	P	L	E
S	P	E	N	T
P	U	M	A	S

Q W E R T Y U I O P
A S D F G H J K L
Z X C V B N M

Clue: harvest

V	E	N	U	E
F	A	L	S	E
B	A	S	E	S

Q W E R T Y U I O P
A S D F G H J K L
Z X C V B N M

Clue: shafts

U	R	B	A	N
L	O	V	E	D
P	R	O	O	F

Q W E R T Y U I O P
A S D F G H J K L
Z X C V B N M

Clue: flecks

J	U	D	G	E
C	L	E	A	R
F	E	R	R	Y

Q W E R T Y U I O P
A S D F G H J K L
Z X C V B N M

Clue: weakens

Puzzle 33

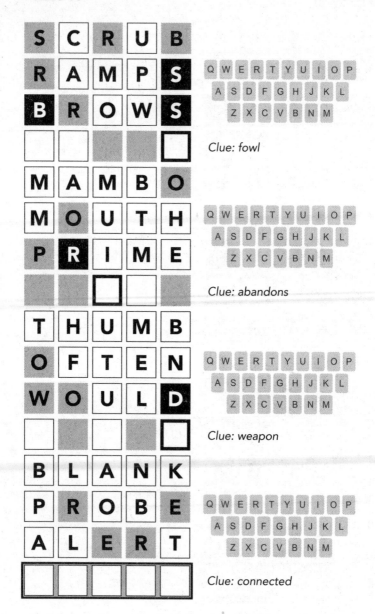

S	C	R	U	B
R	A	M	P	S
B	R	O	W	S

Q W E R T Y U I O P
A S D F G H J K L
Z X C V B N M

Clue: fowl

M	A	M	B	O
M	O	U	T	H
P	R	I	M	E

Q W E R T Y U I O P
A S D F G H J K L
Z X C V B N M

Clue: abandons

T	H	U	M	B
O	F	T	E	N
W	O	U	L	D

Q W E R T Y U I O P
A S D F G H J K L
Z X C V B N M

Clue: weapon

B	L	A	N	K
P	R	O	B	E
A	L	E	R	T

Q W E R T Y U I O P
A S D F G H J K L
Z X C V B N M

Clue: connected

Puzzle 34

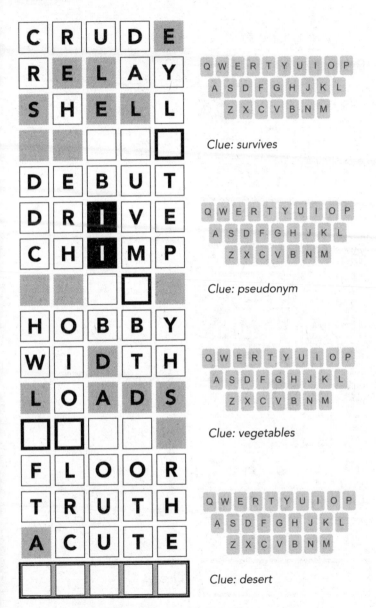

C	R	U	D	E
R	E	L	A	Y
S	H	E	L	L
D	E	B	U	T
D	R	I	V	E
C	H	I	M	P
H	O	B	B	Y
W	I	D	T	H
L	O	A	D	S
F	L	O	O	R
T	R	U	T	H
A	C	U	T	E

Q W E R T Y U I O P
A S D F G H J K L
Z X C V B N M

Clue: survives

Q W E R T Y U I O P
A S D F G H J K L
Z X C V B N M

Clue: pseudonym

Q W E R T Y U I O P
A S D F G H J K L
Z X C V B N M

Clue: vegetables

Q W E R T Y U I O P
A S D F G H J K L
Z X C V B N M

Clue: desert

EASY

Puzzle 35

T	I	G	H	T
F	L	U	I	D
B	A	L	D	Y

Q W E R T Y U I O P
A S D F G H J K L
Z X C V B N M

Clue: register

B	I	R	T	H
S	T	U	F	F
T	W	I	S	T

Q W E R T Y U I O P
A S D F G H J K L
Z X C V B N M

Clue: recordings

F	A	R	M	S
S	H	A	D	E
E	S	S	A	Y

Q W E R T Y U I O P
A S D F G H J K L
Z X C V B N M

Clue: emotional

N	I	G	H	T
B	U	D	D	Y
D	R	Y	E	R

Q W E R T Y U I O P
A S D F G H J K L
Z X C V B N M

Clue: extra

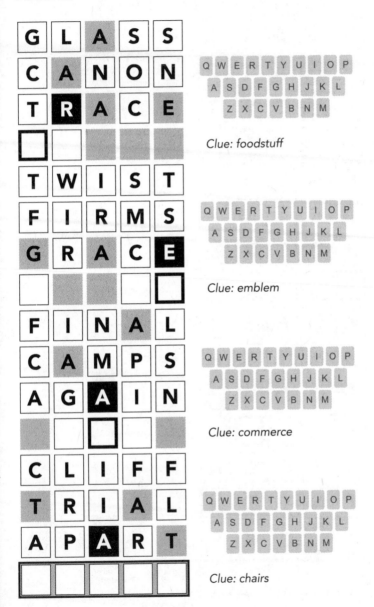

Puzzle 36

G	L	A	S	S
C	A	N	O	N
T	R	A	C	E
T	W	I	S	T
F	I	R	M	S
G	R	A	C	E
F	I	N	A	L
C	A	M	P	S
A	G	A	I	N
C	L	I	F	F
T	R	I	A	L
A	P	A	R	T

Q W E R T Y U I O P
A S D F G H J K L
Z X C V B N M

Clue: foodstuff

Q W E R T Y U I O P
A S D F G H J K L
Z X C V B N M

Clue: emblem

Q W E R T Y U I O P
A S D F G H J K L
Z X C V B N M

Clue: commerce

Q W E R T Y U I O P
A S D F G H J K L
Z X C V B N M

Clue: chairs

EASY

Puzzle 37

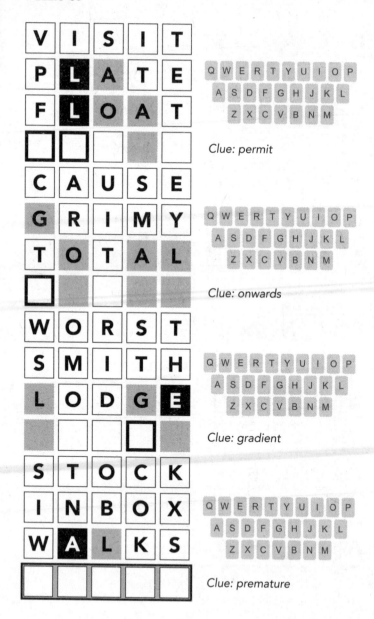

V	I	S	I	T
P	L	A	T	E
F	L	O	A	T

Q W E R T Y U I O P
A S D F G H J K L
Z X C V B N M

Clue: permit

C	A	U	S	E
G	R	I	M	Y
T	O	T	A	L

Q W E R T Y U I O P
A S D F G H J K L
Z X C V B N M

Clue: onwards

W	O	R	S	T
S	M	I	T	H
L	O	D	G	E

Q W E R T Y U I O P
A S D F G H J K L
Z X C V B N M

Clue: gradient

S	T	O	C	K
I	N	B	O	X
W	A	L	K	S

Q W E R T Y U I O P
A S D F G H J K L
Z X C V B N M

Clue: premature

EASY

Puzzle 38

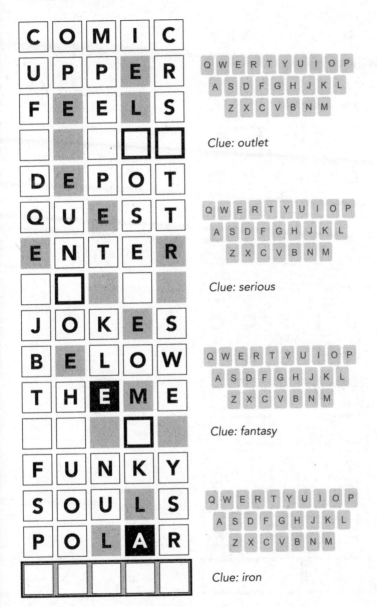

C	O	M	I	C
U	P	P	E	R
F	E	E	L	S

Q W E R T Y U I O P
A S D F G H J K L
Z X C V B N M

Clue: outlet

D	E	P	O	T
Q	U	E	S	T
E	N	T	E	R

Q W E R T Y U I O P
A S D F G H J K L
Z X C V B N M

Clue: serious

J	O	K	E	S
B	E	L	O	W
T	H	E	M	E

Q W E R T Y U I O P
A S D F G H J K L
Z X C V B N M

Clue: fantasy

F	U	N	K	Y
S	O	U	L	S
P	O	L	A	R

Q W E R T Y U I O P
A S D F G H J K L
Z X C V B N M

Clue: iron

Puzzle 39

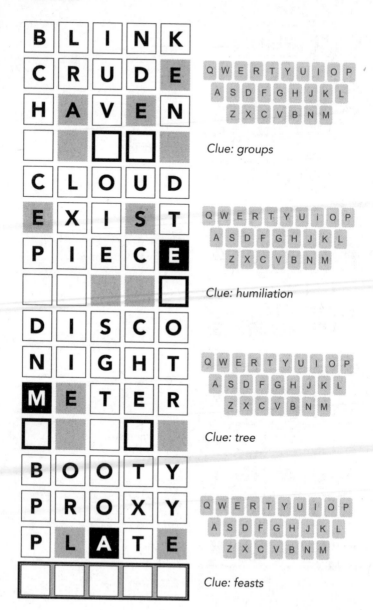

B	L	I	N	K
C	R	U	D	E
H	A	V	E	N
C	L	O	U	D
E	X	I	S	T
P	I	E	C	E
D	I	S	C	O
N	I	G	H	T
M	E	T	E	R
B	O	O	T	Y
P	R	O	X	Y
P	L	A	T	E

Q W E R T Y U I O P
A S D F G H J K L
Z X C V B N M

Clue: groups

Q W E R T Y U I O P
A S D F G H J K L
Z X C V B N M

Clue: humiliation

Q W E R T Y U I O P
A S D F G H J K L
Z X C V B N M

Clue: tree

Q W E R T Y U I O P
A S D F G H J K L
Z X C V B N M

Clue: feasts

Puzzle 40

EASY

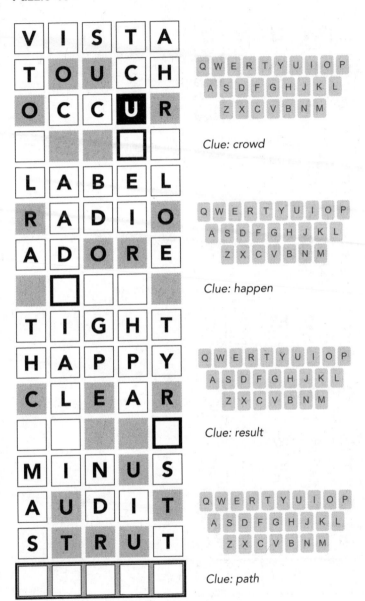

V	I	S	T	A
T	O	U	C	H
O	C	C	U	R
L	A	B	E	L
R	A	D	I	O
A	D	O	R	E
T	I	G	H	T
H	A	P	P	Y
C	L	E	A	R
M	I	N	U	S
A	U	D	I	T
S	T	R	U	T

Q W E R T Y U I O P
A S D F G H J K L
Z X C V B N M

Clue: crowd

Q W E R T Y U I O P
A S D F G H J K L
Z X C V B N M

Clue: happen

Q W E R T Y U I O P
A S D F G H J K L
Z X C V B N M

Clue: result

Q W E R T Y U I O P
A S D F G H J K L
Z X C V B N M

Clue: path

Puzzle 41

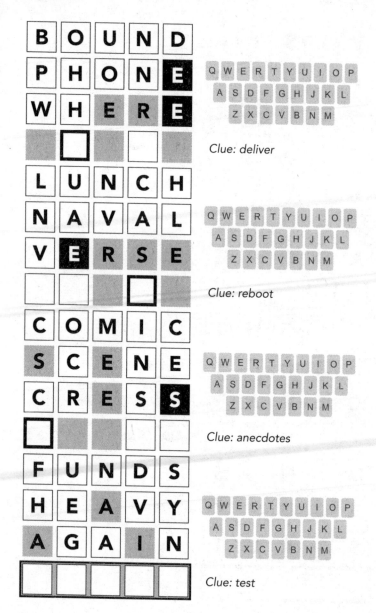

B	O	U	N	D
P	H	O	N	E
W	H	E	R	E
L	U	N	C	H
N	A	V	A	L
V	E	R	S	E
C	O	M	I	C
S	C	E	N	E
C	R	E	S	S
F	U	N	D	S
H	E	A	V	Y
A	G	A	I	N

Q W E R T Y U I O P
A S D F G H J K L
Z X C V B N M

Clue: deliver

Q W E R T Y U I O P
A S D F G H J K L
Z X C V B N M

Clue: reboot

Q W E R T Y U I O P
A S D F G H J K L
Z X C V B N M

Clue: anecdotes

Q W E R T Y U I O P
A S D F G H J K L
Z X C V B N M

Clue: test

EASY

Puzzle 42

S	T	A	F	F
S	O	N	G	S
O	P	E	R	A

Q W E R T Y U I O P
A S D F G H J K L
Z X C V B N M

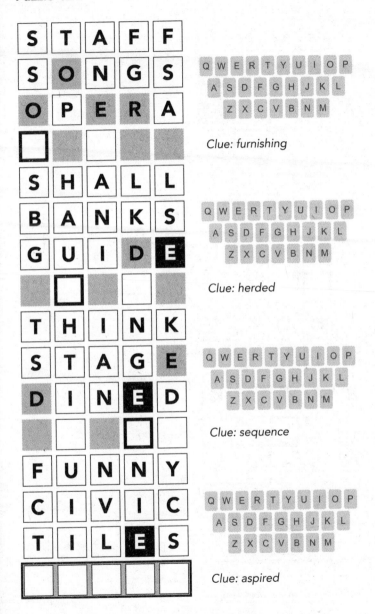

Clue: furnishing

S	H	A	L	L
B	A	N	K	S
G	U	I	D	E

Q W E R T Y U I O P
A S D F G H J K L
Z X C V B N M

Clue: herded

T	H	I	N	K
S	T	A	G	E
D	I	N	E	D

Q W E R T Y U I O P
A S D F G H J K L
Z X C V B N M

Clue: sequence

F	U	N	N	Y
C	I	V	I	C
T	I	L	E	S

Q W E R T Y U I O P
A S D F G H J K L
Z X C V B N M

Clue: aspired

E
A
S
Y

Puzzle 43

O	U	G	H	T
P	A	T	H	S
E	P	I	C	S

Q W E R T Y U I O P
A S D F G H J K L
Z X C V B N M

Clue: blazes

P	R	O	X	Y
A	N	G	R	Y
R	U	R	A	L

Q W E R T Y U I O P
A S D F G H J K L
Z X C V B N M

Clue: protected

S	H	O	T	S
M	I	N	E	R
B	R	E	A	K

Q W E R T Y U I O P
A S D F G H J K L
Z X C V B N M

Clue: big

R	O	C	K	Y
P	R	O	M	O
C	A	R	R	Y

Q W E R T Y U I O P
A S D F G H J K L
Z X C V B N M

Clue: infectious

Puzzle 44

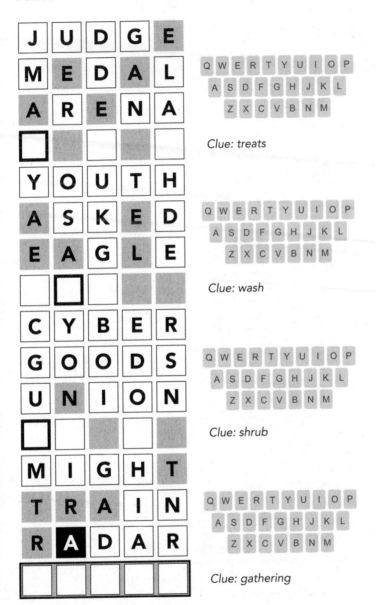

J	U	D	G	E
M	E	D	A	L
A	R	E	N	A

Q W E R T Y U I O P
A S D F G H J K L
Z X C V B N M

Clue: treats

Y	O	U	T	H
A	S	K	E	D
E	A	G	L	E

Q W E R T Y U I O P
A S D F G H J K L
Z X C V B N M

Clue: wash

C	Y	B	E	R
G	O	O	D	S
U	N	I	O	N

Q W E R T Y U I O P
A S D F G H J K L
Z X C V B N M

Clue: shrub

M	I	G	H	T
T	R	A	I	N
R	A	D	A	R

Q W E R T Y U I O P
A S D F G H J K L
Z X C V B N M

Clue: gathering

Puzzle 45

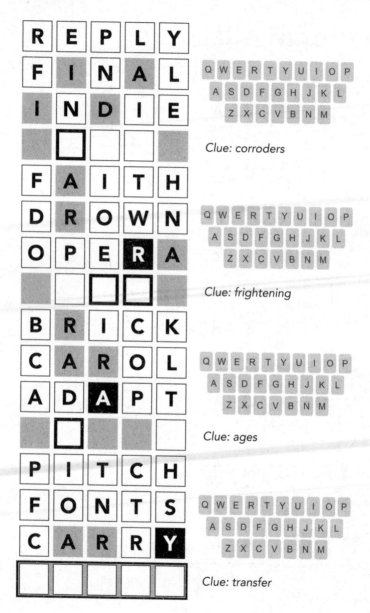

R	E	P	L	Y
F	I	N	A	L
I	N	D	I	E
F	A	I	T	H
D	R	O	W	N
O	P	E	R	A
B	R	I	C	K
C	A	R	O	L
A	D	A	P	T
P	I	T	C	H
F	O	N	T	S
C	A	R	R	Y

Q W E R T Y U I O P
A S D F G H J K L
Z X C V B N M

Clue: corroders

Q W E R T Y U I O P
A S D F G H J K L
Z X C V B N M

Clue: frightening

Q W E R T Y U I O P
A S D F G H J K L
Z X C V B N M

Clue: ages

Q W E R T Y U I O P
A S D F G H J K L
Z X C V B N M

Clue: transfer

Puzzle 46

M	A	R	C	H
B	A	D	L	Y
A	D	D	E	R

Q W E R T Y U I O P
A S D F G H J K L
Z X C V B N M

Clue: rapidity

M	I	G	H	T
W	E	I	R	D
E	A	R	L	Y

Q W E R T Y U I O P
A S D F G H J K L
Z X C V B N M

Clue: board

B	U	N	N	Y
P	R	A	Y	S
E	A	R	T	H

Q W E R T Y U I O P
A S D F G H J K L
Z X C V B N M

Clue: month

Q	U	E	S	T
K	I	T	T	Y
J	U	I	C	E

Q W E R T Y U I O P
A S D F G H J K L
Z X C V B N M

Clue: broadcaster

Puzzle 47

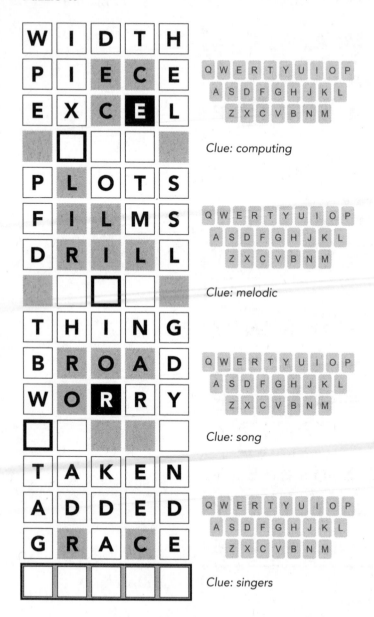

W	I	D	T	H	
P	I	E	C	E	Q W E R T Y U I O P
E	X	C	E	L	A S D F G H J K L
					Z X C V B N M
					Clue: computing
P	L	O	T	S	
F	I	L	M	S	Q W E R T Y U I O P
D	R	I	L	L	A S D F G H J K L
					Z X C V B N M
					Clue: melodic
T	H	I	N	G	
B	R	O	A	D	Q W E R T Y U I O P
W	O	R	R	Y	A S D F G H J K L
					Z X C V B N M
					Clue: song
T	A	K	E	N	
A	D	D	E	D	Q W E R T Y U I O P
G	R	A	C	E	A S D F G H J K L
					Z X C V B N M
					Clue: singers

Puzzle 48

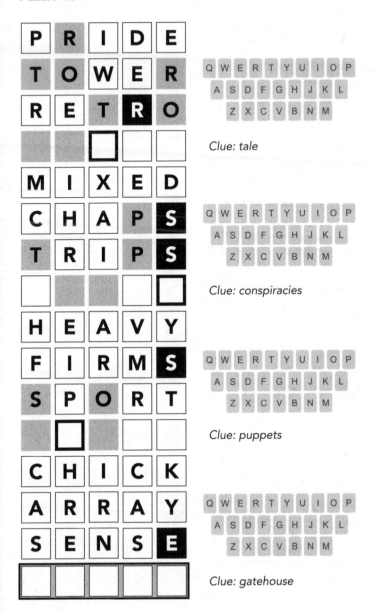

P	R	I	D	E
T	O	W	E	R
R	E	T	R	O

Q W E R T Y U I O P
A S D F G H J K L
Z X C V B N M

Clue: tale

M	I	X	E	D
C	H	A	P	S
T	R	I	P	S

Q W E R T Y U I O P
A S D F G H J K L
Z X C V B N M

Clue: conspiracies

H	E	A	V	Y
F	I	R	M	S
S	P	O	R	T

Q W E R T Y U I O P
A S D F G H J K L
Z X C V B N M

Clue: puppets

C	H	I	C	K
A	R	R	A	Y
S	E	N	S	E

Q W E R T Y U I O P
A S D F G H J K L
Z X C V B N M

Clue: gatehouse

E
A
S
Y

Puzzle 49

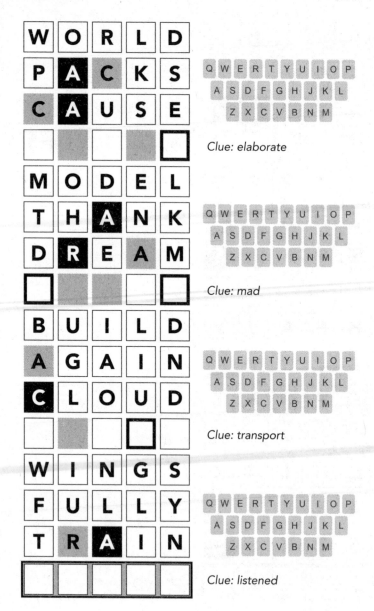

W	O	R	L	D
P	A	C	K	S
C	A	U	S	E
M	O	D	E	L
T	H	A	N	K
D	R	E	A	M
B	U	I	L	D
A	G	A	I	N
C	L	O	U	D
W	I	N	G	S
F	U	L	L	Y
T	R	A	I	N

Q W E R T Y U I O P
A S D F G H J K L
Z X C V B N M

Clue: elaborate

Q W E R T Y U I O P
A S D F G H J K L
Z X C V B N M

Clue: mad

Q W E R T Y U I O P
A S D F G H J K L
Z X C V B N M

Clue: transport

Q W E R T Y U I O P
A S D F G H J K L
Z X C V B N M

Clue: listened

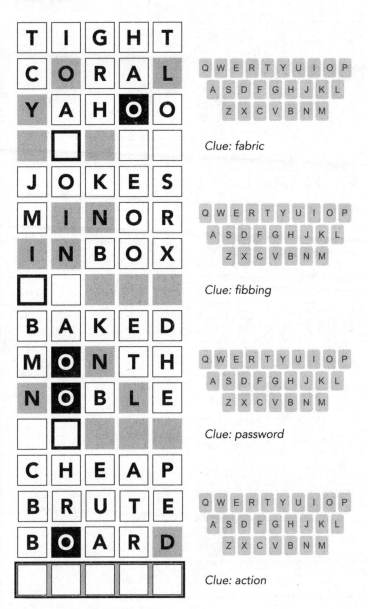

Puzzle 50

EASY

T	I	G	H	T
C	O	R	A	L
Y	A	H	O	O
J	O	K	E	S
M	I	N	O	R
I	N	B	O	X
B	A	K	E	D
M	O	N	T	H
N	O	B	L	E
C	H	E	A	P
B	R	U	T	E
B	O	A	R	D

Q W E R T Y U I O P
A S D F G H J K L
Z X C V B N M

Clue: fabric

Q W E R T Y U I O P
A S D F G H J K L
Z X C V B N M

Clue: fibbing

Q W E R T Y U I O P
A S D F G H J K L
Z X C V B N M

Clue: password

Q W E R T Y U I O P
A S D F G H J K L
Z X C V B N M

Clue: action

EASY

Puzzle 51

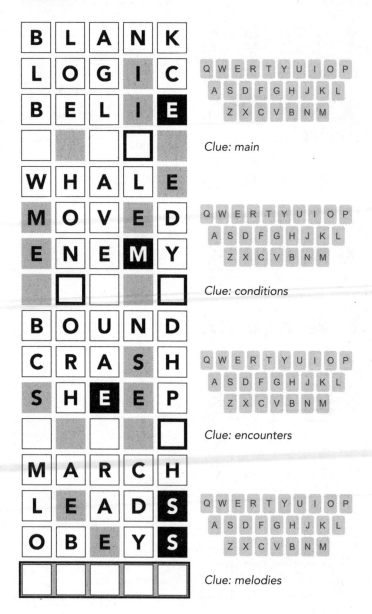

B	L	A	N	K
L	O	G	I	C
B	E	L	I	E

Q W E R T Y U I O P
A S D F G H J K L
Z X C V B N M

Clue: main

W	H	A	L	E
M	O	V	E	D
E	N	E	M	Y

Q W E R T Y U I O P
A S D F G H J K L
Z X C V B N M

Clue: conditions

B	O	U	N	D
C	R	A	S	H
S	H	E	E	P

Q W E R T Y U I O P
A S D F G H J K L
Z X C V B N M

Clue: encounters

M	A	R	C	H
L	E	A	D	S
O	B	E	Y	S

Q W E R T Y U I O P
A S D F G H J K L
Z X C V B N M

Clue: melodies

Puzzle 52

K	I	N	D	S
P	A	S	T	E
S	H	I	R	T

QWERTYUIOP
ASDFGHJKL
ZXCVBNM

Clue: expedition

K	A	R	M	A
Q	U	O	T	E
G	U	E	S	T

QWERTYUIOP
ASDFGHJKL
ZXCVBNM

Clue: cylinders

M	A	T	C	H
B	U	D	G	E
S	E	E	R	S

QWERTYUIOP
ASDFGHJKL
ZXCVBNM

Clue: protest

F	U	N	N	Y
W	I	N	E	S
F	L	E	E	T

QWERTYUIOP
ASDFGHJKL
ZXCVBNM

Clue: elude

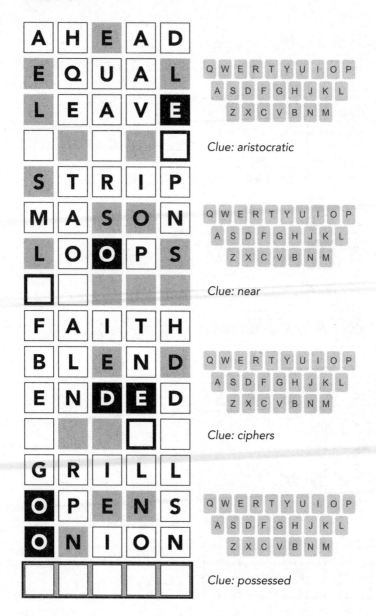

EASY

Puzzle 53

A	H	E	A	D
E	Q	U	A	L
L	E	A	V	E
S	T	R	I	P
M	A	S	O	N
L	O	O	P	S
F	A	I	T	H
B	L	E	N	D
E	N	D	E	D
G	R	I	L	L
O	P	E	N	S
O	N	I	O	N

Q W E R T Y U I O P
A S D F G H J K L
Z X C V B N M

Clue: aristocratic

Q W E R T Y U I O P
A S D F G H J K L
Z X C V B N M

Clue: near

Q W E R T Y U I O P
A S D F G H J K L
Z X C V B N M

Clue: ciphers

Q W E R T Y U I O P
A S D F G H J K L
Z X C V B N M

Clue: possessed

Puzzle 54

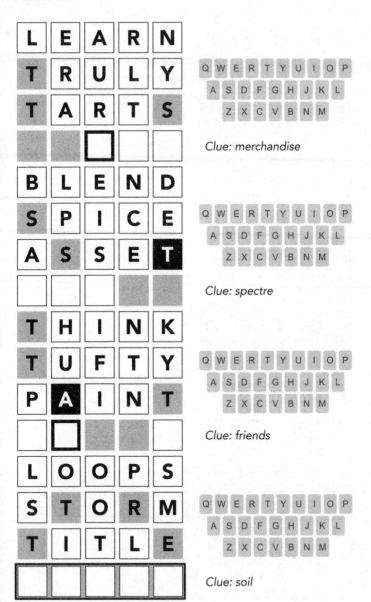

L	E	A	R	N
T	R	U	L	Y
T	A	R	T	S

Q W E R T Y U I O P
A S D F G H J K L
Z X C V B N M

Clue: merchandise

B	L	E	N	D
S	P	I	C	E
A	S	S	E	T

Q W E R T Y U I O P
A S D F G H J K L
Z X C V B N M

Clue: spectre

T	H	I	N	K
T	U	F	T	Y
P	A	I	N	T

Q W E R T Y U I O P
A S D F G H J K L
Z X C V B N M

Clue: friends

L	O	O	P	S
S	T	O	R	M
T	I	T	L	E

Q W E R T Y U I O P
A S D F G H J K L
Z X C V B N M

Clue: soil

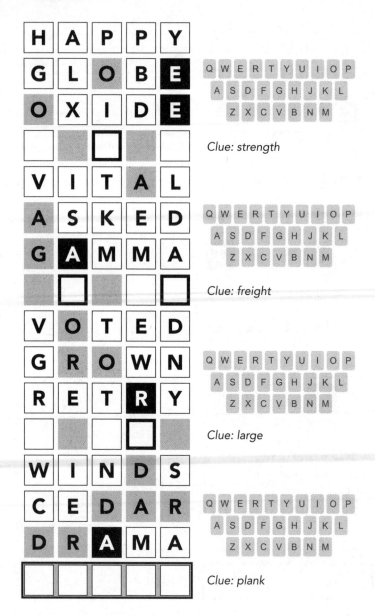

EASY

Puzzle 55

H	A	P	P	Y
G	L	O	B	E
O	X	I	D	E

Q W E R T Y U I O P
A S D F G H J K L
Z X C V B N M

Clue: strength

V	I	T	A	L
A	S	K	E	D
G	A	M	M	A

Q W E R T Y U I O P
A S D F G H J K L
Z X C V B N M

Clue: freight

V	O	T	E	D
G	R	O	W	N
R	E	T	R	Y

Q W E R T Y U I O P
A S D F G H J K L
Z X C V B N M

Clue: large

W	I	N	D	S
C	E	D	A	R
D	R	A	M	A

Q W E R T Y U I O P
A S D F G H J K L
Z X C V B N M

Clue: plank

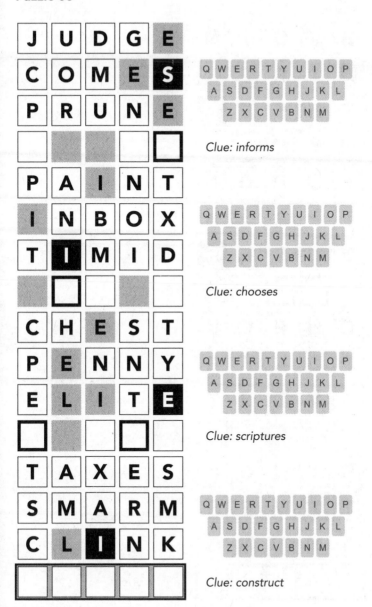

Puzzle 56

J	U	D	G	E
C	O	M	E	S
P	R	U	N	E
P	A	I	N	T
I	N	B	O	X
T	I	M	I	D
C	H	E	S	T
P	E	N	N	Y
E	L	I	T	E
T	A	X	E	S
S	M	A	R	M
C	L	I	N	K

Q W E R T Y U I O P
A S D F G H J K L
Z X C V B N M

Clue: informs

Q W E R T Y U I O P
A S D F G H J K L
Z X C V B N M

Clue: chooses

Q W E R T Y U I O P
A S D F G H J K L
Z X C V B N M

Clue: scriptures

Q W E R T Y U I O P
A S D F G H J K L
Z X C V B N M

Clue: construct

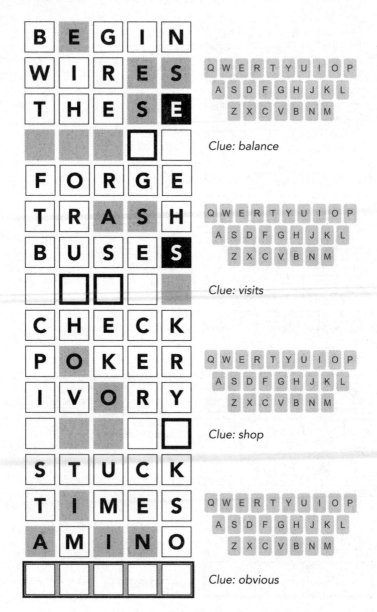

EASY

Puzzle 57

B	E	G	I	N	
W	I	R	E	S	Q W E R T Y U I O P A S D F G H J K L Z X C V B N M
T	H	E	S	E	
					Clue: *balance*
F	O	R	G	E	
T	R	A	S	H	Q W E R T Y U I O P A S D F G H J K L Z X C V B N M
B	U	S	E	S	
					Clue: *visits*
C	H	E	C	K	
P	O	K	E	R	Q W E R T Y U I O P A S D F G H J K L Z X C V B N M
I	V	O	R	Y	
					Clue: *shop*
S	T	U	C	K	
T	I	M	E	S	Q W E R T Y U I O P A S D F G H J K L Z X C V B N M
A	M	I	N	O	
					Clue: *obvious*

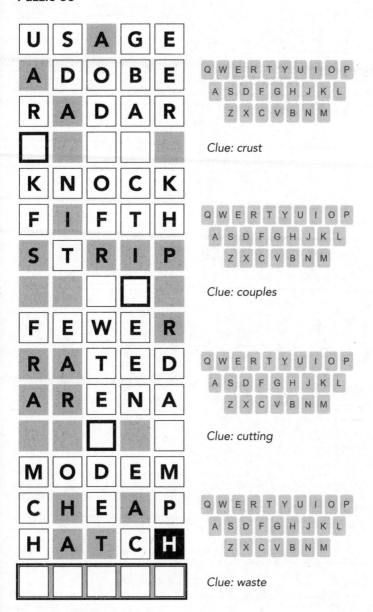

Puzzle 58

U	S	A	G	E
A	D	O	B	E
R	A	D	A	R
K	N	O	C	K
F	I	F	T	H
S	T	R	I	P
F	E	W	E	R
R	A	T	E	D
A	R	E	N	A
M	O	D	E	M
C	H	E	A	P
H	A	T	C	H

Q W E R T Y U I O P
A S D F G H J K L
Z X C V B N M

Clue: crust

Q W E R T Y U I O P
A S D F G H J K L
Z X C V B N M

Clue: couples

Q W E R T Y U I O P
A S D F G H J K L
Z X C V B N M

Clue: cutting

Q W E R T Y U I O P
A S D F G H J K L
Z X C V B N M

Clue: waste

EASY

Puzzle 59

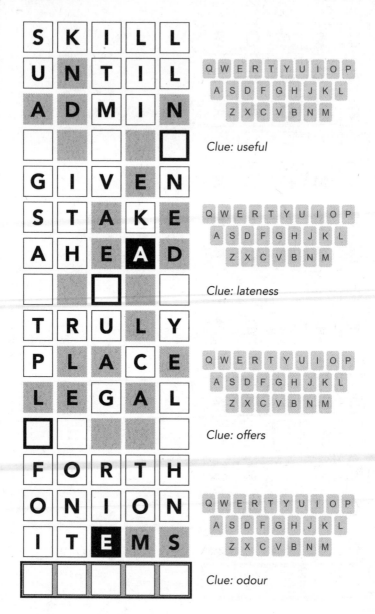

S	K	I	L	L
U	N	T	I	L
A	D	M	I	N
G	I	V	E	N
S	T	A	K	E
A	H	E	A	D
T	R	U	L	Y
P	L	A	C	E
L	E	G	A	L
F	O	R	T	H
O	N	I	O	N
I	T	E	M	S

Q W E R T Y U I O P
A S D F G H J K L
Z X C V B N M

Clue: useful

Q W E R T Y U I O P
A S D F G H J K L
Z X C V B N M

Clue: lateness

Q W E R T Y U I O P
A S D F G H J K L
Z X C V B N M

Clue: offers

Q W E R T Y U I O P
A S D F G H J K L
Z X C V B N M

Clue: odour

Puzzle 60

E	X	A	M	S
H	O	O	D	Y
T	O	D	A	Y
L	U	C	K	Y
V	I	N	Y	L
I	N	N	E	R
T	R	E	E	S
W	A	L	K	S
B	R	A	N	D
T	R	U	N	K
H	O	N	E	Y
N	E	R	V	E

Q W E R T Y U I O P
A S D F G H J K L
Z X C V B N M

Clue: cart

Q W E R T Y U I O P
A S D F G H J K L
Z X C V B N M

Clue: profits

Q W E R T Y U I O P
A S D F G H J K L
Z X C V B N M

Clue: between

Q W E R T Y U I O P
A S D F G H J K L
Z X C V B N M

Clue: cartoons

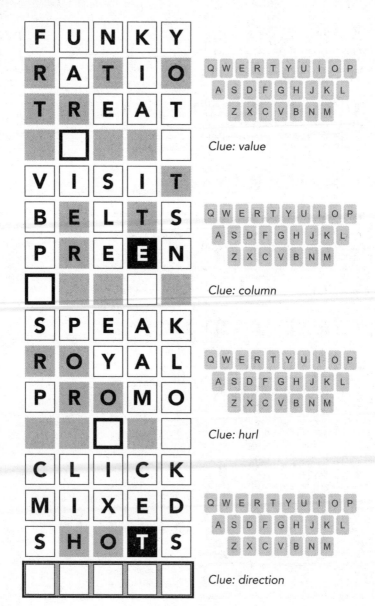

Puzzle 61

F	U	N	K	Y
R	A	T	I	O
T	R	E	A	T

Q W E R T Y U I O P
A S D F G H J K L
Z X C V B N M

Clue: value

V	I	S	I	T
B	E	L	T	S
P	R	E	E	N

Q W E R T Y U I O P
A S D F G H J K L
Z X C V B N M

Clue: column

S	P	E	A	K
R	O	Y	A	L
P	R	O	M	O

Q W E R T Y U I O P
A S D F G H J K L
Z X C V B N M

Clue: hurl

C	L	I	C	K
M	I	X	E	D
S	H	O	T	S

Q W E R T Y U I O P
A S D F G H J K L
Z X C V B N M

Clue: direction

Puzzle 62

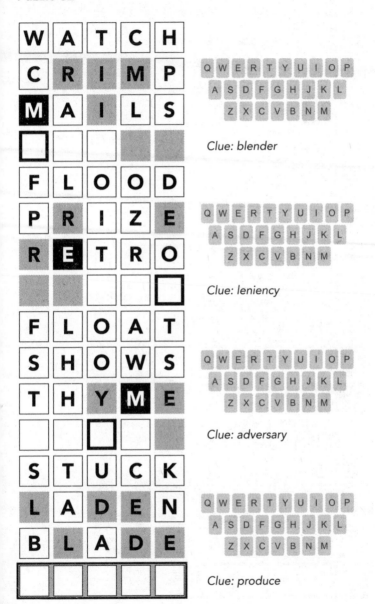

W	A	T	C	H
C	R	I	M	P
M	A	I	L	S

QWERTYUIOP
ASDFGHJKL
ZXCVBNM

Clue: blender

F	L	O	O	D
P	R	I	Z	E
R	E	T	R	O

QWERTYUIOP
ASDFGHJKL
ZXCVBNM

Clue: leniency

F	L	O	A	T
S	H	O	W	S
T	H	Y	M	E

QWERTYUIOP
ASDFGHJKL
ZXCVBNM

Clue: adversary

S	T	U	C	K
L	A	D	E	N
B	L	A	D	E

QWERTYUIOP
ASDFGHJKL
ZXCVBNM

Clue: produce

EASY

Puzzle 63

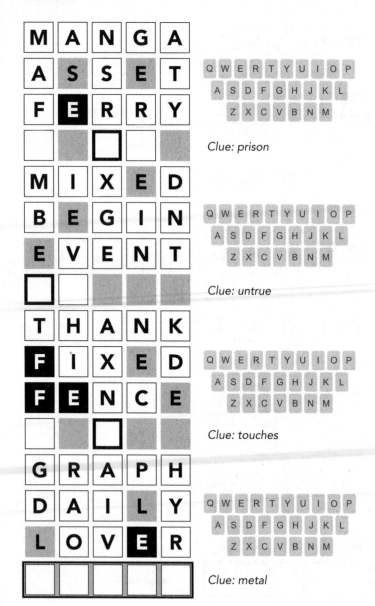

M	A	N	G	A
A	S	S	E	T
F	E	R	R	Y

QWERTYUIOP
ASDFGHJKL
ZXCVBNM

Clue: prison

M	I	X	E	D
B	E	G	I	N
E	V	E	N	T

QWERTYUIOP
ASDFGHJKL
ZXCVBNM

Clue: untrue

T	H	A	N	K
F	I	X	E	D
F	E	N	C	E

QWERTYUIOP
ASDFGHJKL
ZXCVBNM

Clue: touches

G	R	A	P	H
D	A	I	L	Y
L	O	V	E	R

QWERTYUIOP
ASDFGHJKL
ZXCVBNM

Clue: metal

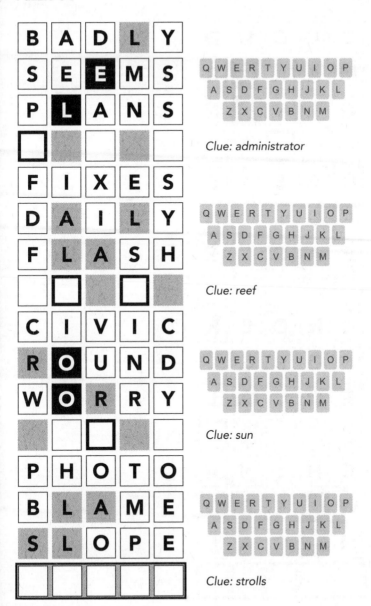

Puzzle 64

EASY

B	A	D	L	Y
S	E	E	M	S
P	L	A	N	S
F	I	X	E	S
D	A	I	L	Y
F	L	A	S	H
C	I	V	I	C
R	O	U	N	D
W	O	R	R	Y
P	H	O	T	O
B	L	A	M	E
S	L	O	P	E

Q W E R T Y U I O P
A S D F G H J K L
Z X C V B N M

Clue: administrator

Q W E R T Y U I O P
A S D F G H J K L
Z X C V B N M

Clue: reef

Q W E R T Y U I O P
A S D F G H J K L
Z X C V B N M

Clue: sun

Q W E R T Y U I O P
A S D F G H J K L
Z X C V B N M

Clue: strolls

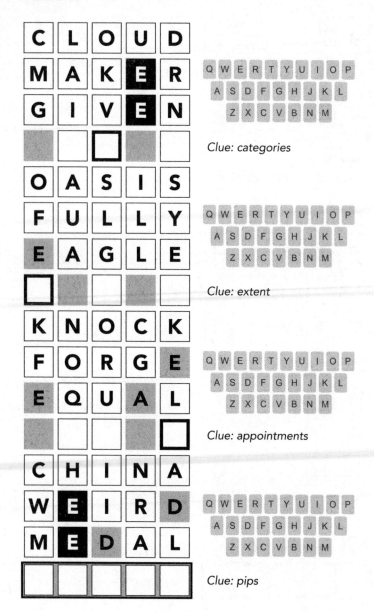

Puzzle 65

C	L	O	U	D
M	A	K	E	R
G	I	V	E	N

Q W E R T Y U I O P
A S D F G H J K L
Z X C V B N M

Clue: categories

O	A	S	I	S
F	U	L	L	Y
E	A	G	L	E

Q W E R T Y U I O P
A S D F G H J K L
Z X C V B N M

Clue: extent

K	N	O	C	K
F	O	R	G	E
E	Q	U	A	L

Q W E R T Y U I O P
A S D F G H J K L
Z X C V B N M

Clue: appointments

C	H	I	N	A
W	E	I	R	D
M	E	D	A	L

Q W E R T Y U I O P
A S D F G H J K L
Z X C V B N M

Clue: pips

Puzzle 66

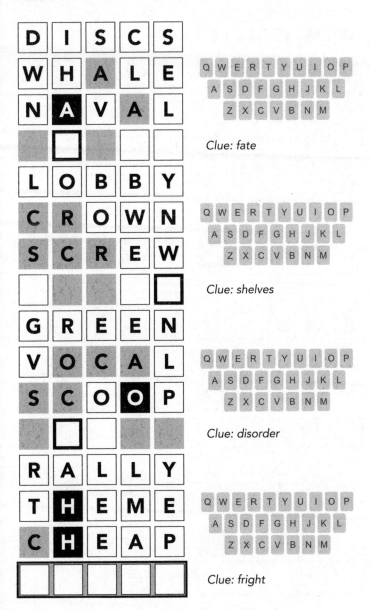

D	I	S	C	S
W	H	A	L	E
N	A	V	A	L
L	O	B	B	Y
C	R	O	W	N
S	C	R	E	W
G	R	E	E	N
V	O	C	A	L
S	C	O	O	P
R	A	L	L	Y
T	H	E	M	E
C	H	E	A	P

Q W E R T Y U I O P
A S D F G H J K L
Z X C V B N M

Clue: fate

Q W E R T Y U I O P
A S D F G H J K L
Z X C V B N M

Clue: shelves

Q W E R T Y U I O P
A S D F G H J K L
Z X C V B N M

Clue: disorder

Q W E R T Y U I O P
A S D F G H J K L
Z X C V B N M

Clue: fright

EASY

Puzzle 67

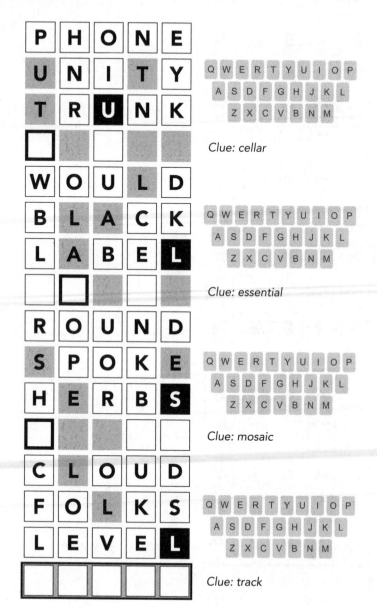

P	H	O	N	E	
U	N	I	T	Y	Q W E R T Y U I O P / A S D F G H J K L / Z X C V B N M
T	R	U	N	K	
					Clue: cellar
W	O	U	L	D	
B	L	A	C	K	Q W E R T Y U I O P / A S D F G H J K L / Z X C V B N M
L	A	B	E	L	
					Clue: essential
R	O	U	N	D	
S	P	O	K	E	Q W E R T Y U I O P / A S D F G H J K L / Z X C V B N M
H	E	R	B	S	
					Clue: mosaic
C	L	O	U	D	
F	O	L	K	S	Q W E R T Y U I O P / A S D F G H J K L / Z X C V B N M
L	E	V	E	L	
					Clue: track

EASY

Puzzle 68

F	O	U	N	D
Q	U	E	R	Y
K	E	E	P	S
C	A	T	C	H
O	A	S	I	S
B	O	O	S	T
A	D	M	I	N
P	U	N	C	H
P	O	L	L	S
P	A	S	T	A
F	I	F	T	Y
H	O	N	E	Y

Q W E R T Y U I O P
A S D F G H J K L
Z X C V B N M

Clue: gardens

Q W E R T Y U I O P
A S D F G H J K L
Z X C V B N M

Clue: talked

Q W E R T Y U I O P
A S D F G H J K L
Z X C V B N M

Clue: reader

Q W E R T Y U I O P
A S D F G H J K L
Z X C V B N M

Clue: underneath

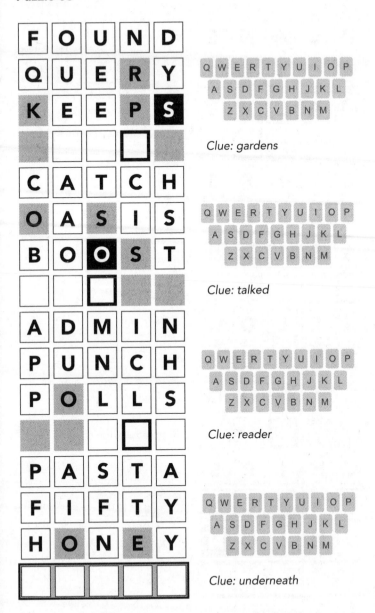

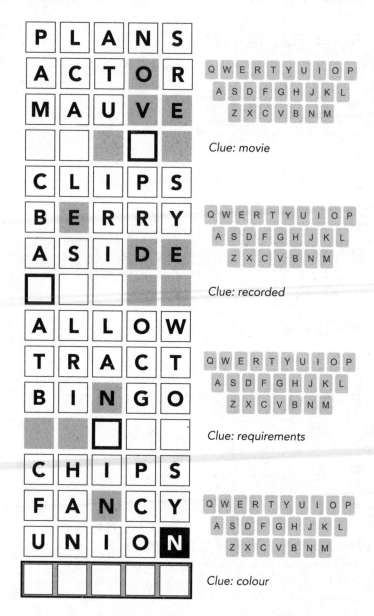

EASY

Puzzle 69

P	L	A	N	S
A	C	T	O	R
M	A	U	V	E

Q W E R T Y U I O P
A S D F G H J K L
Z X C V B N M

Clue: movie

C	L	I	P	S
B	E	R	R	Y
A	S	I	D	E

Q W E R T Y U I O P
A S D F G H J K L
Z X C V B N M

Clue: recorded

A	L	L	O	W
T	R	A	C	T
B	I	N	G	O

Q W E R T Y U I O P
A S D F G H J K L
Z X C V B N M

Clue: requirements

C	H	I	P	S
F	A	N	C	Y
U	N	I	O	N

Q W E R T Y U I O P
A S D F G H J K L
Z X C V B N M

Clue: colour

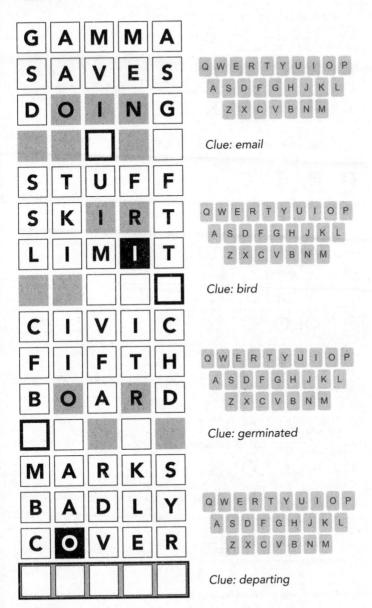

Puzzle 70

EASY

G	A	M	M	A
S	A	V	E	S
D	O	I	N	G

Q W E R T Y U I O P
A S D F G H J K L
Z X C V B N M

Clue: email

S	T	U	F	F
S	K	I	R	T
L	I	M	I	T

Q W E R T Y U I O P
A S D F G H J K L
Z X C V B N M

Clue: bird

C	I	V	I	C
F	I	F	T	H
B	O	A	R	D

Q W E R T Y U I O P
A S D F G H J K L
Z X C V B N M

Clue: germinated

M	A	R	K	S
B	A	D	L	Y
C	O	V	E	R

Q W E R T Y U I O P
A S D F G H J K L
Z X C V B N M

Clue: departing

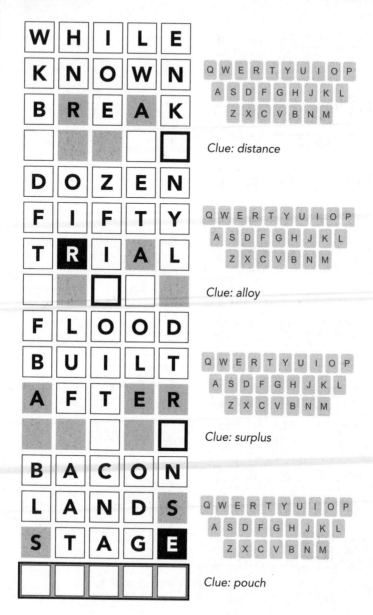

EASY

Puzzle 71

W	H	I	L	E
K	N	O	W	N
B	R	E	A	K
D	O	Z	E	N
F	I	F	T	Y
T	R	I	A	L
F	L	O	O	D
B	U	I	L	T
A	F	T	E	R
B	A	C	O	N
L	A	N	D	S
S	T	A	G	E

Q W E R T Y U I O P
A S D F G H J K L
Z X C V B N M

Clue: distance

Q W E R T Y U I O P
A S D F G H J K L
Z X C V B N M

Clue: alloy

Q W E R T Y U I O P
A S D F G H J K L
Z X C V B N M

Clue: surplus

Q W E R T Y U I O P
A S D F G H J K L
Z X C V B N M

Clue: pouch

Puzzle 72

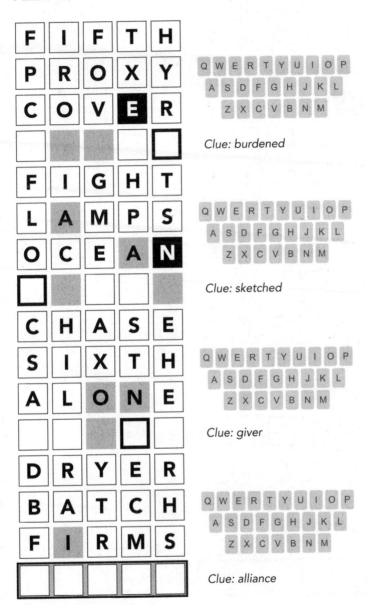

F	I	F	T	H
P	R	O	X	Y
C	O	V	E	R

Q W E R T Y U I O P
A S D F G H J K L
Z X C V B N M

Clue: burdened

F	I	G	H	T
L	A	M	P	S
O	C	E	A	N

Q W E R T Y U I O P
A S D F G H J K L
Z X C V B N M

Clue: sketched

C	H	A	S	E
S	I	X	T	H
A	L	O	N	E

Q W E R T Y U I O P
A S D F G H J K L
Z X C V B N M

Clue: giver

D	R	Y	E	R
B	A	T	C	H
F	I	R	M	S

Q W E R T Y U I O P
A S D F G H J K L
Z X C V B N M

Clue: alliance

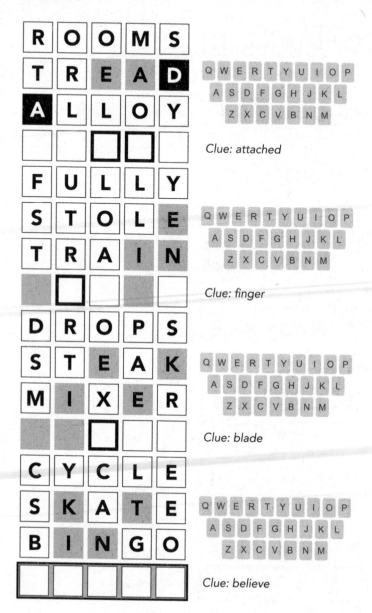

Puzzle 73

R	O	O	M	S
T	R	E	A	D
A	L	L	O	Y

QWERTYUIOP
ASDFGHJKL
ZXCVBNM

Clue: attached

F	U	L	L	Y
S	T	O	L	E
T	R	A	I	N

QWERTYUIOP
ASDFGHJKL
ZXCVBNM

Clue: finger

D	R	O	P	S
S	T	E	A	K
M	I	X	E	R

QWERTYUIOP
ASDFGHJKL
ZXCVBNM

Clue: blade

C	Y	C	L	E
S	K	A	T	E
B	I	N	G	O

QWERTYUIOP
ASDFGHJKL
ZXCVBNM

Clue: believe

Puzzle 74

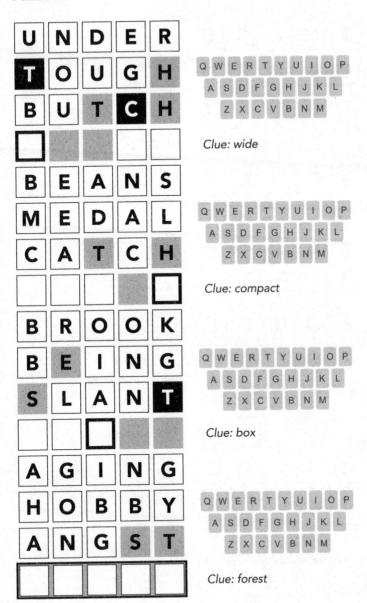

U	N	D	E	R
T	O	U	G	H
B	U	T	C	H

Q W E R T Y U I O P
A S D F G H J K L
Z X C V B N M

Clue: wide

B	E	A	N	S
M	E	D	A	L
C	A	T	C	H

Q W E R T Y U I O P
A S D F G H J K L
Z X C V B N M

Clue: compact

B	R	O	O	K
B	E	I	N	G
S	L	A	N	T

Q W E R T Y U I O P
A S D F G H J K L
Z X C V B N M

Clue: box

A	G	I	N	G
H	O	B	B	Y
A	N	G	S	T

Q W E R T Y U I O P
A S D F G H J K L
Z X C V B N M

Clue: forest

EASY

Puzzle 75

T	H	E	S	E	
F	I	R	E	D	Q W E R T Y U I O P A S D F G H J K L Z X C V B N M
F	A	N	C	Y	
					Clue: plain
Z	O	N	E	S	
M	I	G	H	T	Q W E R T Y U I O P A S D F G H J K L Z X C V B N M
T	R	A	C	E	
					Clue: poorly
R	O	U	G	E	
F	O	C	U	S	Q W E R T Y U I O P A S D F G H J K L Z X C V B N M
M	E	D	A	L	
					Clue: correct
H	E	L	L	O	
B	U	C	K	S	Q W E R T Y U I O P A S D F G H J K L Z X C V B N M
P	I	L	O	T	
					Clue: exhaust

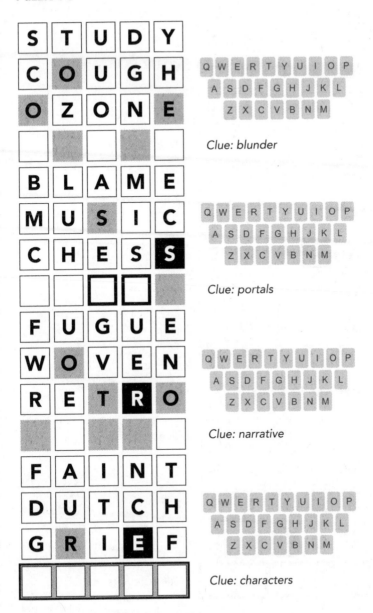

Puzzle 76

S	T	U	D	Y
C	O	U	G	H
O	Z	O	N	E

Q W E R T Y U I O P
A S D F G H J K L
Z X C V B N M

Clue: blunder

B	L	A	M	E
M	U	S	I	C
C	H	E	S	S

Q W E R T Y U I O P
A S D F G H J K L
Z X C V B N M

Clue: portals

F	U	G	U	E
W	O	V	E	N
R	E	T	R	O

Q W E R T Y U I O P
A S D F G H J K L
Z X C V B N M

Clue: narrative

F	A	I	N	T
D	U	T	C	H
G	R	I	E	F

Q W E R T Y U I O P
A S D F G H J K L
Z X C V B N M

Clue: characters

MEDIUM

Puzzle 77

MEDIUM

M	A	T	C	H	
R	E	C	U	T	
S	W	E	A	T	
					Clue: *packed*
T	A	L	L	Y	
G	U	S	T	Y	
M	E	R	G	E	
					Clue: *creature*
C	R	A	W	L	
I	N	F	E	R	
E	K	I	N	G	
					Clue: *estimate*
M	O	D	A	L	
S	T	A	F	F	
M	O	I	S	T	
					Clue: *attempts*

Q W E R T Y U I O P
A S D F G H J K L
Z X C V B N M

Q W E R T Y U I O P
A S D F G H J K L
Z X C V B N M

Q W E R T Y U I O P
A S D F G H J K L
Z X C V B N M

Q W E R T Y U I O P
A S D F G H J K L
Z X C V B N M

Puzzle 78

A	L	L	O	T
C	L	A	S	H
V	I	C	A	R

Q W E R T Y U I O P
A S D F G H J K L
Z X C V B N M

Clue: sacked

I	C	I	N	G
P	U	N	C	H
T	H	Y	M	E

Q W E R T Y U I O P
A S D F G H J K L
Z X C V B N M

Clue: attempt

W	R	I	S	T
S	N	I	F	F
A	V	O	I	D

Q W E R T Y U I O P
A S D F G H J K L
Z X C V B N M

Clue: cooked

C	O	U	N	T
F	O	L	L	Y
R	A	N	C	H

Q W E R T Y U I O P
A S D F G H J K L
Z X C V B N M

Clue: perceived

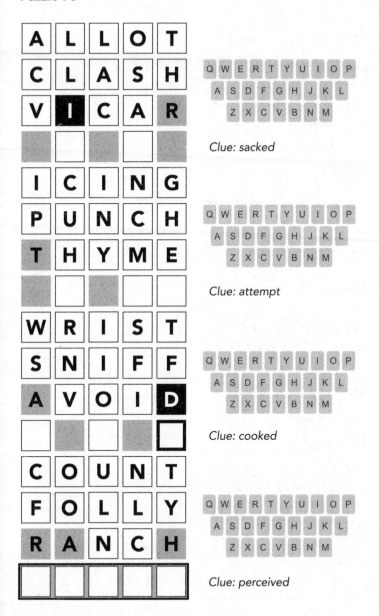

MEDIUM

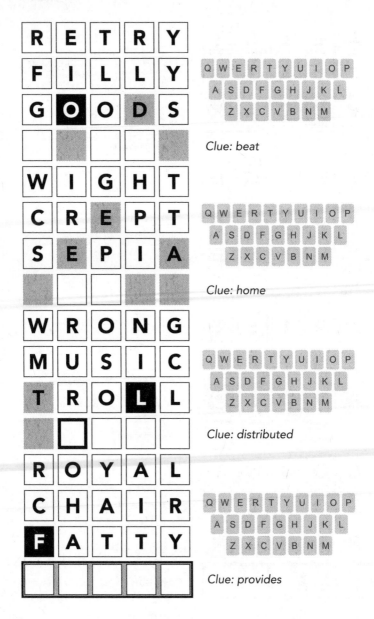

MEDIUM

Puzzle 79

R	E	T	R	Y
F	I	L	L	Y
G	O	O	D	S

Q W E R T Y U I O P
A S D F G H J K L
Z X C V B N M

Clue: beat

W	I	G	H	T
C	R	E	P	T
S	E	P	I	A

Q W E R T Y U I O P
A S D F G H J K L
Z X C V B N M

Clue: home

W	R	O	N	G
M	U	S	I	C
T	R	O	L	L

Q W E R T Y U I O P
A S D F G H J K L
Z X C V B N M

Clue: distributed

R	O	Y	A	L
C	H	A	I	R
F	A	T	T	Y

Q W E R T Y U I O P
A S D F G H J K L
Z X C V B N M

Clue: provides

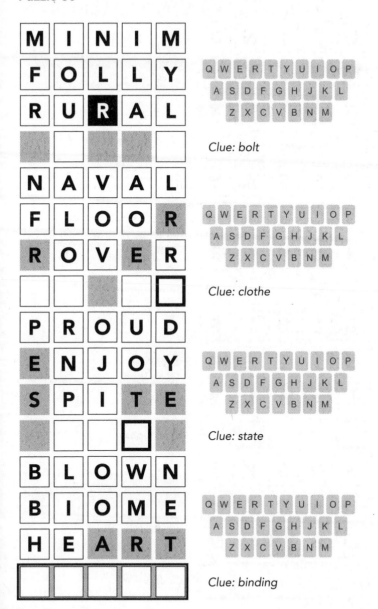

Puzzle 80

M	I	N	I	M
F	O	L	L	Y
R	U	R	A	L
N	A	V	A	L
F	L	O	O	R
R	O	V	E	R
P	R	O	U	D
E	N	J	O	Y
S	P	I	T	E
B	L	O	W	N
B	I	O	M	E
H	E	A	R	T

Q W E R T Y U I O P
A S D F G H J K L
Z X C V B N M

Clue: bolt

Q W E R T Y U I O P
A S D F G H J K L
Z X C V B N M

Clue: clothe

Q W E R T Y U I O P
A S D F G H J K L
Z X C V B N M

Clue: state

Q W E R T Y U I O P
A S D F G H J K L
Z X C V B N M

Clue: binding

MEDIUM

Puzzle 81

MEDIUM

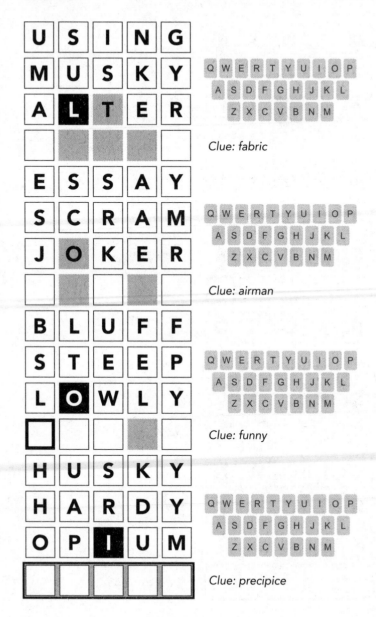

U	S	I	N	G
M	U	S	K	Y
A	L	T	E	R

Q W E R T Y U I O P
A S D F G H J K L
Z X C V B N M

Clue: fabric

E	S	S	A	Y
S	C	R	A	M
J	O	K	E	R

Q W E R T Y U I O P
A S D F G H J K L
Z X C V B N M

Clue: airman

B	L	U	F	F
S	T	E	E	P
L	O	W	L	Y

Q W E R T Y U I O P
A S D F G H J K L
Z X C V B N M

Clue: funny

H	U	S	K	Y
H	A	R	D	Y
O	P	I	U	M

Q W E R T Y U I O P
A S D F G H J K L
Z X C V B N M

Clue: precipice

Puzzle 82

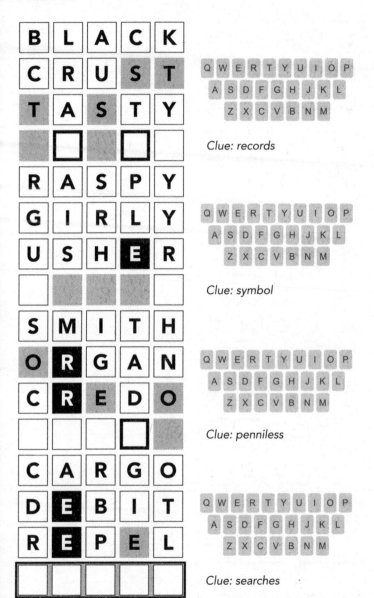

B	L	A	C	K
C	R	U	S	T
T	A	S	T	Y
R	A	S	P	Y
G	I	R	L	Y
U	S	H	E	R
S	M	I	T	H
O	R	G	A	N
C	R	E	D	O
C	A	R	G	O
D	E	B	I	T
R	E	P	E	L

Q W E R T Y U I O P
A S D F G H J K L
Z X C V B N M

Clue: records

Q W E R T Y U I O P
A S D F G H J K L
Z X C V B N M

Clue: symbol

Q W E R T Y U I O P
A S D F G H J K L
Z X C V B N M

Clue: penniless

Q W E R T Y U I O P
A S D F G H J K L
Z X C V B N M

Clue: searches

MEDIUM

MEDIUM

Puzzle 83

S	O	U	T	H	
D	O	N	O	R	QWERTYUIOP / ASDFGHJKL / ZXCVBNM
V	E	R	S	O	
					Clue: award
W	I	T	T	Y	
A	D	A	P	T	QWERTYUIOP / ASDFGHJKL / ZXCVBNM
N	O	M	A	D	
					Clue: mount
A	L	O	N	G	
S	N	A	R	E	QWERTYUIOP / ASDFGHJKL / ZXCVBNM
R	I	S	E	R	
					Clue: confidence
P	A	D	D	Y	
A	L	L	E	Y	QWERTYUIOP / ASDFGHJKL / ZXCVBNM
P	R	A	W	N	
					Clue: split

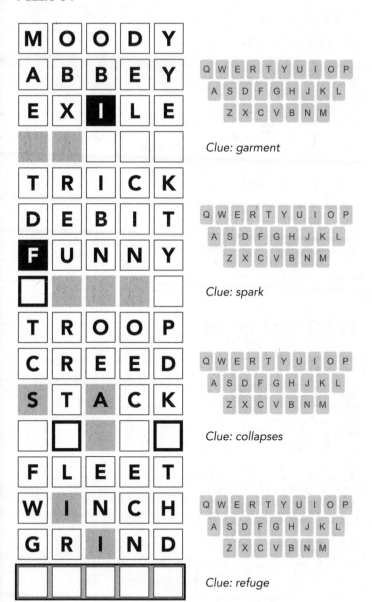

Puzzle 84

M	O	O	D	Y	
A	B	B	E	Y	Q W E R T Y U I O P
E	X	I	L	E	A S D F G H J K L / Z X C V B N M
					Clue: *garment*
T	R	I	C	K	
D	E	B	I	T	Q W E R T Y U I O P
F	U	N	N	Y	A S D F G H J K L / Z X C V B N M
					Clue: *spark*
T	R	O	O	P	
C	R	E	E	D	Q W E R T Y U I O P
S	T	A	C	K	A S D F G H J K L / Z X C V B N M
					Clue: *collapses*
F	L	E	E	T	
W	I	N	C	H	Q W E R T Y U I O P
G	R	I	N	D	A S D F G H J K L / Z X C V B N M
					Clue: *refuge*

MEDIUM

MEDIUM

Puzzle 85

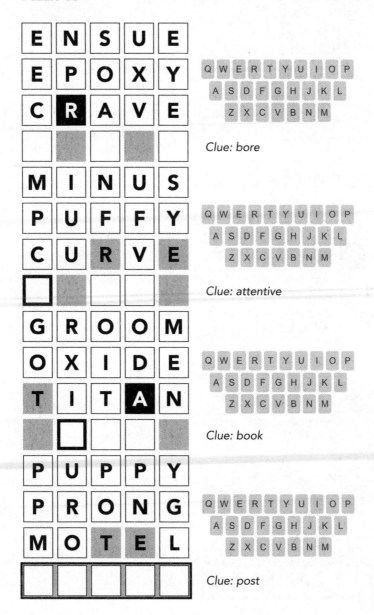

E	N	S	U	E	
E	P	O	X	Y	
C	R	A	V	E	
					Clue: bore
M	I	N	U	S	
P	U	F	F	Y	
C	U	R	V	E	
					Clue: attentive
G	R	O	O	M	
O	X	I	D	E	
T	I	T	A	N	
					Clue: book
P	U	P	P	Y	
P	R	O	N	G	
M	O	T	E	L	
					Clue: post

Q W E R T Y U I O P
A S D F G H J K L
Z X C V B N M

Q W E R T Y U I O P
A S D F G H J K L
Z X C V B N M

Q W E R T Y U I O P
A S D F G H J K L
Z X C V B N M

Q W E R T Y U I O P
A S D F G H J K L
Z X C V B N M

Puzzle 86

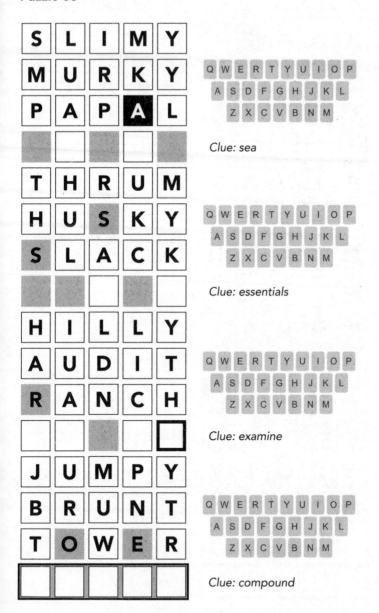

S	L	I	M	Y
M	U	R	K	Y
P	A	P	A	L

Q W E R T Y U I O P
A S D F G H J K L
Z X C V B N M

Clue: sea

T	H	R	U	M
H	U	S	K	Y
S	L	A	C	K

Q W E R T Y U I O P
A S D F G H J K L
Z X C V B N M

Clue: essentials

H	I	L	L	Y
A	U	D	I	T
R	A	N	C	H

Q W E R T Y U I O P
A S D F G H J K L
Z X C V B N M

Clue: examine

J	U	M	P	Y
B	R	U	N	T
T	O	W	E	R

Q W E R T Y U I O P
A S D F G H J K L
Z X C V B N M

Clue: compound

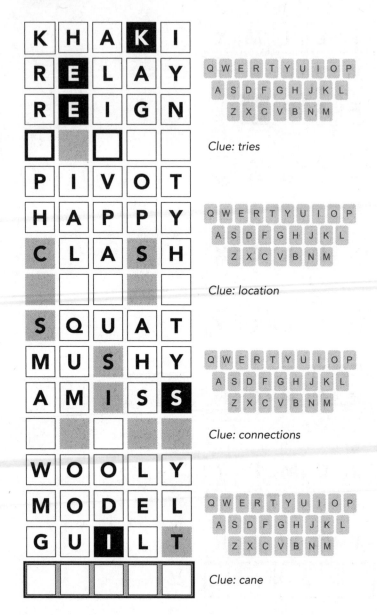

MEDIUM

Puzzle 87

K	H	A	K	I
R	E	L	A	Y
R	E	I	G	N

Q W E R T Y U I O P
A S D F G H J K L
Z X C V B N M

Clue: tries

P	I	V	O	T
H	A	P	P	Y
C	L	A	S	H

Q W E R T Y U I O P
A S D F G H J K L
Z X C V B N M

Clue: location

S	Q	U	A	T
M	U	S	H	Y
A	M	I	S	S

Q W E R T Y U I O P
A S D F G H J K L
Z X C V B N M

Clue: connections

W	O	O	L	Y
M	O	D	E	L
G	U	I	L	T

Q W E R T Y U I O P
A S D F G H J K L
Z X C V B N M

Clue: cane

Puzzle 88

I	D	I	O	T
S	L	O	T	H
J	U	I	C	E

Q W E R T Y U I O P
A S D F G H J K L
Z X C V B N M

Clue: cool

G	L	O	B	E
W	I	S	E	R
D	A	L	L	Y

Q W E R T Y U I O P
A S D F G H J K L
Z X C V B N M

Clue: mortal

R	E	F	E	R
S	L	O	P	E
D	R	A	M	A

Q W E R T Y U I O P
A S D F G H J K L
Z X C V B N M

Clue: comic

G	E	N	R	E
A	S	I	D	E
S	H	A	K	E

Q W E R T Y U I O P
A S D F G H J K L
Z X C V B N M

Clue: nearby

MEDIUM

Puzzle 89

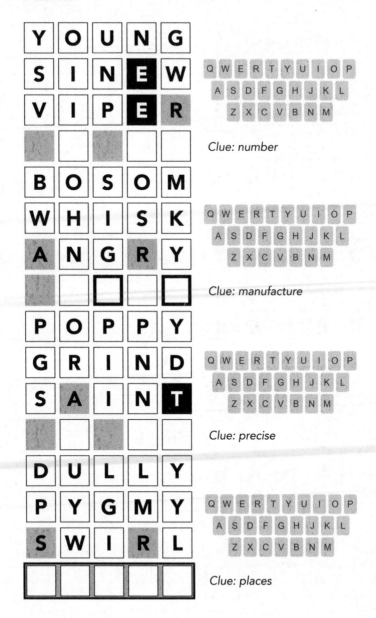

MEDIUM

Y	O	U	N	G
S	I	N	E	W
V	I	P	E	R

Q W E R T Y U I O P
A S D F G H J K L
Z X C V B N M

Clue: number

B	O	S	O	M
W	H	I	S	K
A	N	G	R	Y

Q W E R T Y U I O P
A S D F G H J K L
Z X C V B N M

Clue: manufacture

P	O	P	P	Y
G	R	I	N	D
S	A	I	N	T

Q W E R T Y U I O P
A S D F G H J K L
Z X C V B N M

Clue: precise

D	U	L	L	Y
P	Y	G	M	Y
S	W	I	R	L

Q W E R T Y U I O P
A S D F G H J K L
Z X C V B N M

Clue: places

Puzzle 90

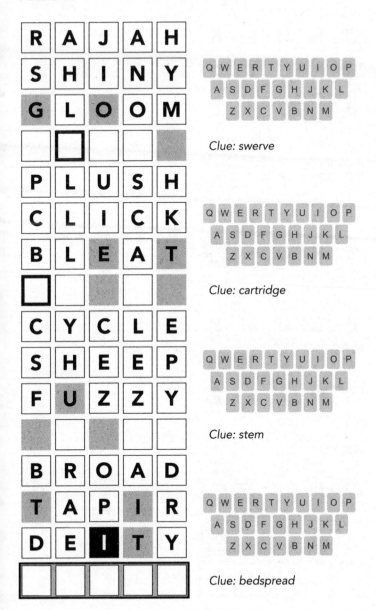

R	A	J	A	H
S	H	I	N	Y
G	L	O	O	M
P	L	U	S	H
C	L	I	C	K
B	L	E	A	T
C	Y	C	L	E
S	H	E	E	P
F	U	Z	Z	Y
B	R	O	A	D
T	A	P	I	R
D	E	I	T	Y

Q W E R T Y U I O P
A S D F G H J K L
Z X C V B N M

Clue: swerve

Q W E R T Y U I O P
A S D F G H J K L
Z X C V B N M

Clue: cartridge

Q W E R T Y U I O P
A S D F G H J K L
Z X C V B N M

Clue: stem

Q W E R T Y U I O P
A S D F G H J K L
Z X C V B N M

Clue: bedspread

MEDIUM

Puzzle 91

D	R	U	N	K
S	N	U	F	F
B	A	S	I	L

Q W E R T Y U I O P
A S D F G H J K L
Z X C V B N M

Clue: sports

T	R	I	C	K
B	R	A	W	N
G	R	O	P	E

Q W E R T Y U I O P
A S D F G H J K L
Z X C V B N M

Clue: residence

P	L	U	M	P
E	N	E	M	A
S	N	A	K	E

Q W E R T Y U I O P
A S D F G H J K L
Z X C V B N M

Clue: situated

H	E	A	R	T
S	T	O	M	P
A	M	I	S	S

Q W E R T Y U I O P
A S D F G H J K L
Z X C V B N M

Clue: brains

Puzzle 92

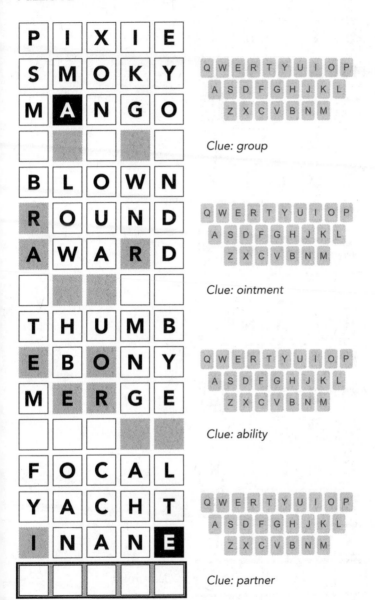

P	I	X	I	E
S	M	O	K	Y
M	A	N	G	O
B	L	O	W	N
R	O	U	N	D
A	W	A	R	D
T	H	U	M	B
E	B	O	N	Y
M	E	R	G	E
F	O	C	A	L
Y	A	C	H	T
I	N	A	N	E

Q W E R T Y U I O P
A S D F G H J K L
Z X C V B N M

Clue: group

Q W E R T Y U I O P
A S D F G H J K L
Z X C V B N M

Clue: ointment

Q W E R T Y U I O P
A S D F G H J K L
Z X C V B N M

Clue: ability

Q W E R T Y U I O P
A S D F G H J K L
Z X C V B N M

Clue: partner

MEDIUM

Puzzle 93

MEDIUM

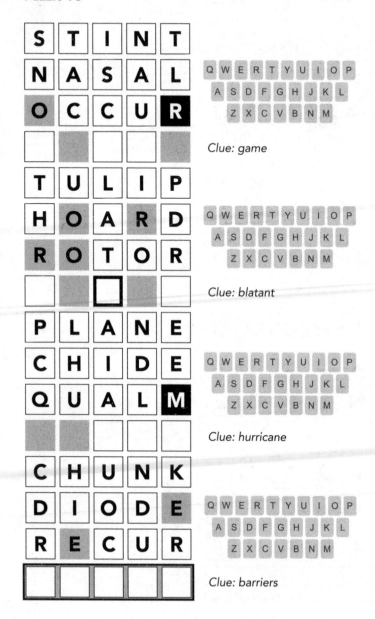

S	T	I	N	T
N	A	S	A	L
O	C	C	U	R

QWERTYUIOP
ASDFGHJKL
ZXCVBNM

Clue: game

T	U	L	I	P
H	O	A	R	D
R	O	T	O	R

QWERTYUIOP
ASDFGHJKL
ZXCVBNM

Clue: blatant

P	L	A	N	E
C	H	I	D	E
Q	U	A	L	M

QWERTYUIOP
ASDFGHJKL
ZXCVBNM

Clue: hurricane

C	H	U	N	K
D	I	O	D	E
R	E	C	U	R

QWERTYUIOP
ASDFGHJKL
ZXCVBNM

Clue: barriers

Puzzle 94

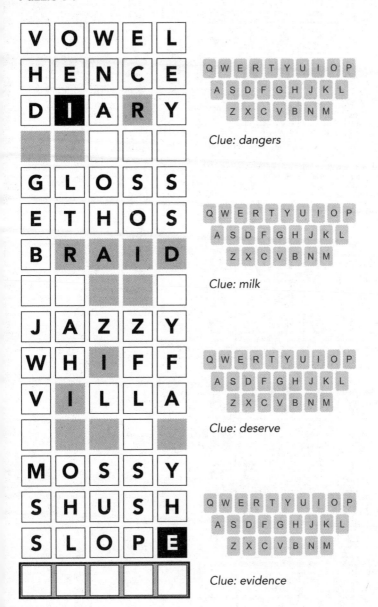

V	O	W	E	L
H	E	N	C	E
D	I	A	R	Y

Q W E R T Y U I O P
A S D F G H J K L
Z X C V B N M

Clue: dangers

G	L	O	S	S
E	T	H	O	S
B	R	A	I	D

Q W E R T Y U I O P
A S D F G H J K L
Z X C V B N M

Clue: milk

J	A	Z	Z	Y
W	H	I	F	F
V	I	L	L	A

Q W E R T Y U I O P
A S D F G H J K L
Z X C V B N M

Clue: deserve

M	O	S	S	Y
S	H	U	S	H
S	L	O	P	E

Q W E R T Y U I O P
A S D F G H J K L
Z X C V B N M

Clue: evidence

MEDIUM

Puzzle 95

MEDIUM

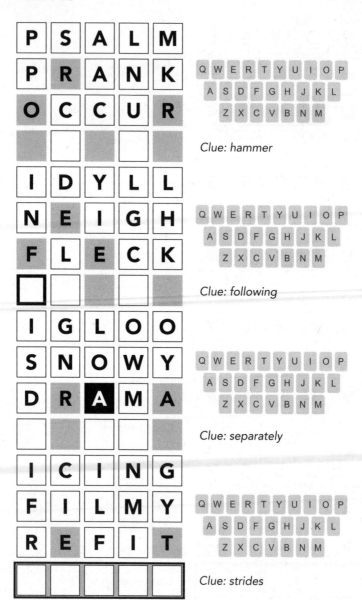

P	S	A	L	M
P	R	A	N	K
O	C	C	U	R

Q W E R T Y U I O P
A S D F G H J K L
Z X C V B N M

Clue: hammer

I	D	Y	L	L
N	E	I	G	H
F	L	E	C	K

Q W E R T Y U I O P
A S D F G H J K L
Z X C V B N M

Clue: following

I	G	L	O	O
S	N	O	W	Y
D	R	A	M	A

Q W E R T Y U I O P
A S D F G H J K L
Z X C V B N M

Clue: separately

I	C	I	N	G
F	I	L	M	Y
R	E	F	I	T

Q W E R T Y U I O P
A S D F G H J K L
Z X C V B N M

Clue: strides

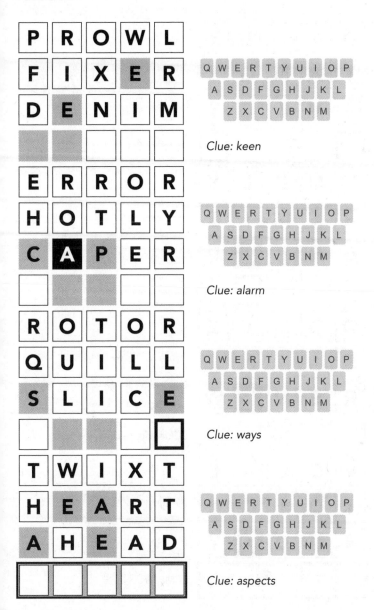

Puzzle 96

P	R	O	W	L
F	I	X	E	R
D	E	N	I	M
E	R	R	O	R
H	O	T	L	Y
C	A	P	E	R
R	O	T	O	R
Q	U	I	L	L
S	L	I	C	E
T	W	I	X	T
H	E	A	R	T
A	H	E	A	D

Q W E R T Y U I O P
A S D F G H J K L
Z X C V B N M

Clue: keen

Q W E R T Y U I O P
A S D F G H J K L
Z X C V B N M

Clue: alarm

Q W E R T Y U I O P
A S D F G H J K L
Z X C V B N M

Clue: ways

Q W E R T Y U I O P
A S D F G H J K L
Z X C V B N M

Clue: aspects

MEDIUM

Puzzle 97

MEDIUM

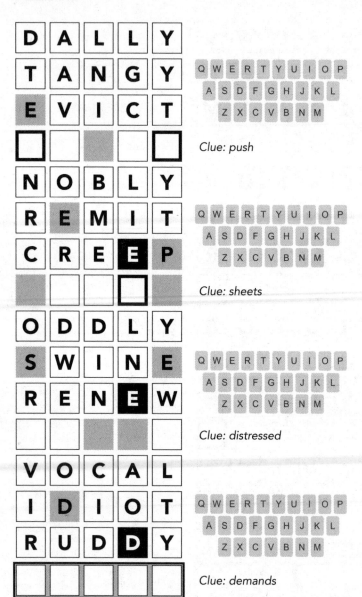

D A L L Y

T A N G Y

QWERTYUIOP
ASDFGHJKL
ZXCVBNM

E V I C T

_ _ _ _ _

Clue: push

N O B L Y

R E M I T

QWERTYUIOP
ASDFGHJKL
ZXCVBNM

C R E E P

_ _ _ _ _

Clue: sheets

O D D L Y

S W I N E

QWERTYUIOP
ASDFGHJKL
ZXCVBNM

R E N E W

_ _ _ _ _

Clue: distressed

V O C A L

I D I O T

QWERTYUIOP
ASDFGHJKL
ZXCVBNM

R U D D Y

_ _ _ _ _

Clue: demands

Puzzle 98

K	N	A	C	K
T	U	B	E	R
W	I	T	T	Y
L	A	T	C	H
G	U	S	T	O
G	L	O	S	S
T	U	N	I	C
P	A	G	A	N
Z	E	S	T	Y
C	H	U	C	K
B	O	U	N	D
P	E	R	K	Y

Q W E R T Y U I O P
A S D F G H J K L
Z X C V B N M

Clue: coldness

Q W E R T Y U I O P
A S D F G H J K L
Z X C V B N M

Clue: functions

Q W E R T Y U I O P
A S D F G H J K L
Z X C V B N M

Clue: elderly

Q W E R T Y U I O P
A S D F G H J K L
Z X C V B N M

Clue: bird

MEDIUM

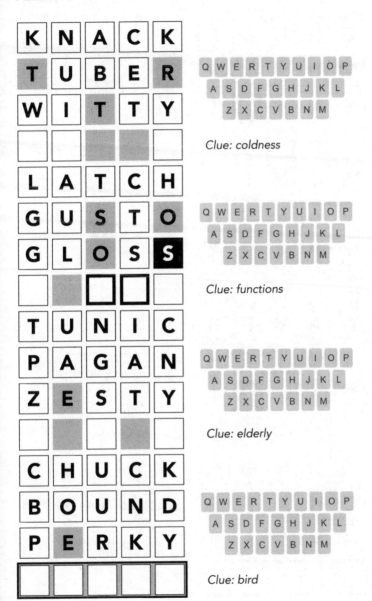

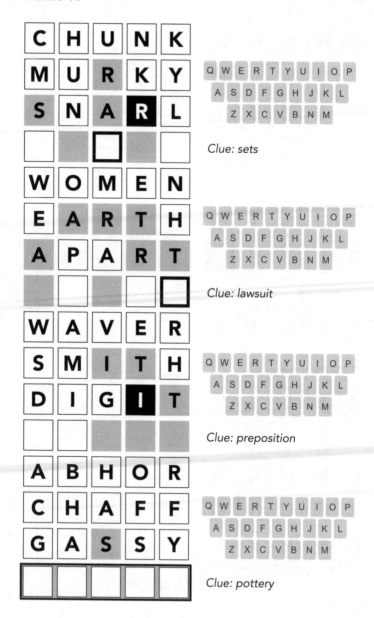

MEDIUM

Puzzle 99

C	H	U	N	K
M	U	R	K	Y
S	N	A	R	L

Q W E R T Y U I O P
A S D F G H J K L
Z X C V B N M

Clue: sets

W	O	M	E	N
E	A	R	T	H
A	P	A	R	T

Q W E R T Y U I O P
A S D F G H J K L
Z X C V B N M

Clue: lawsuit

W	A	V	E	R
S	M	I	T	H
D	I	G	I	T

Q W E R T Y U I O P
A S D F G H J K L
Z X C V B N M

Clue: preposition

A	B	H	O	R
C	H	A	F	F
G	A	S	S	Y

Q W E R T Y U I O P
A S D F G H J K L
Z X C V B N M

Clue: pottery

Puzzle 100

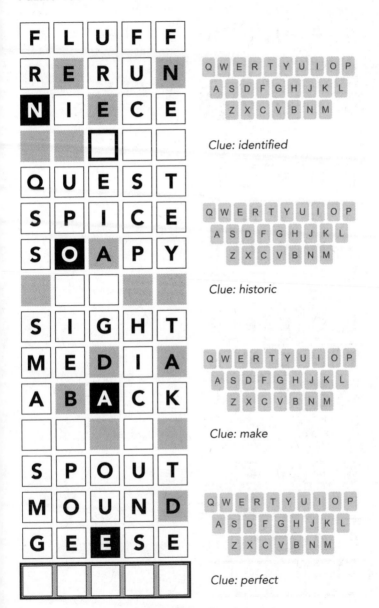

F	L	U	F	F
R	E	R	U	N
N	I	E	C	E
Q	U	E	S	T
S	P	I	C	E
S	O	A	P	Y
S	I	G	H	T
M	E	D	I	A
A	B	A	C	K
S	P	O	U	T
M	O	U	N	D
G	E	E	S	E

Q W E R T Y U I O P
A S D F G H J K L
Z X C V B N M

Clue: identified

Q W E R T Y U I O P
A S D F G H J K L
Z X C V B N M

Clue: historic

Q W E R T Y U I O P
A S D F G H J K L
Z X C V B N M

Clue: make

Q W E R T Y U I O P
A S D F G H J K L
Z X C V B N M

Clue: perfect

MEDIUM

Puzzle 101

MEDIUM

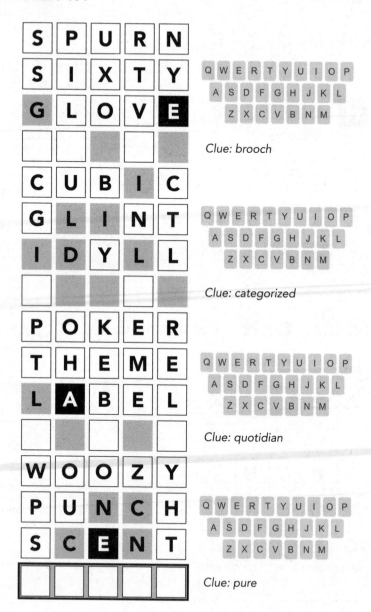

S	P	U	R	N
S	I	X	T	Y
G	L	O	V	E

Q W E R T Y U I O P
A S D F G H J K L
Z X C V B N M

Clue: brooch

C	U	B	I	C
G	L	I	N	T
I	D	Y	L	L

Q W E R T Y U I O P
A S D F G H J K L
Z X C V B N M

Clue: categorized

P	O	K	E	R
T	H	E	M	E
L	A	B	E	L

Q W E R T Y U I O P
A S D F G H J K L
Z X C V B N M

Clue: quotidian

W	O	O	Z	Y
P	U	N	C	H
S	C	E	N	T

Q W E R T Y U I O P
A S D F G H J K L
Z X C V B N M

Clue: pure

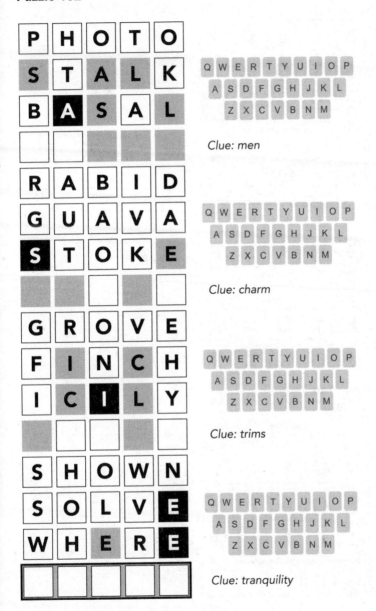

Puzzle 102

P	H	O	T	O
S	T	A	L	K
B	A	S	A	L
R	A	B	I	D
G	U	A	V	A
S	T	O	K	E
G	R	O	V	E
F	I	N	C	H
I	C	I	L	Y
S	H	O	W	N
S	O	L	V	E
W	H	E	R	E

Q W E R T Y U I O P
A S D F G H J K L
Z X C V B N M

Clue: men

Q W E R T Y U I O P
A S D F G H J K L
Z X C V B N M

Clue: charm

Q W E R T Y U I O P
A S D F G H J K L
Z X C V B N M

Clue: trims

Q W E R T Y U I O P
A S D F G H J K L
Z X C V B N M

Clue: tranquility

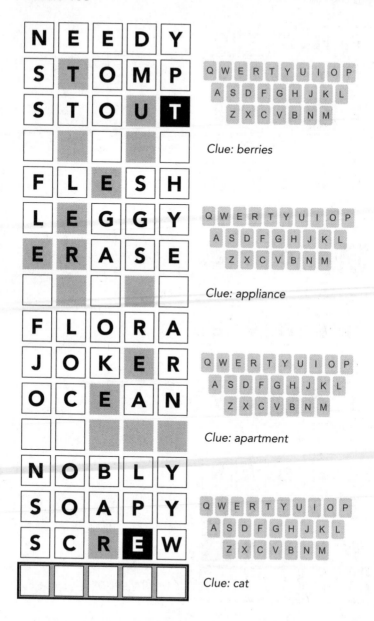

MEDIUM

Puzzle 103

N	E	E	D	Y
S	T	O	M	P
S	T	O	U	T

Q W E R T Y U I O P
A S D F G H J K L
Z X C V B N M

Clue: berries

F	L	E	S	H
L	E	G	G	Y
E	R	A	S	E

Q W E R T Y U I O P
A S D F G H J K L
Z X C V B N M

Clue: appliance

F	L	O	R	A
J	O	K	E	R
O	C	E	A	N

Q W E R T Y U I O P
A S D F G H J K L
Z X C V B N M

Clue: apartment

N	O	B	L	Y
S	O	A	P	Y
S	C	R	E	W

Q W E R T Y U I O P
A S D F G H J K L
Z X C V B N M

Clue: cat

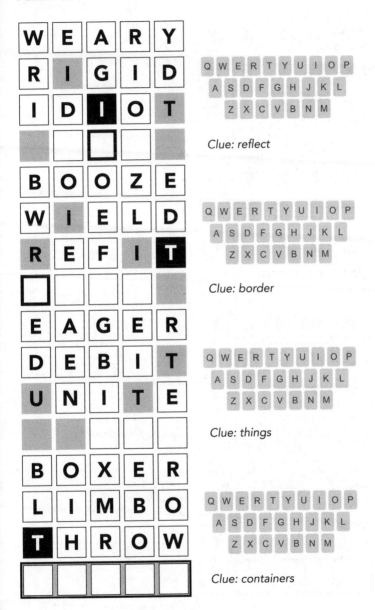

Puzzle 104

W	E	A	R	Y
R	I	G	I	D
I	D	I	O	T

Q W E R T Y U I O P
A S D F G H J K L
Z X C V B N M

Clue: reflect

B	O	O	Z	E
W	I	E	L	D
R	E	F	I	T

Q W E R T Y U I O P
A S D F G H J K L
Z X C V B N M

Clue: border

E	A	G	E	R
D	E	B	I	T
U	N	I	T	E

Q W E R T Y U I O P
A S D F G H J K L
Z X C V B N M

Clue: things

B	O	X	E	R
L	I	M	B	O
T	H	R	O	W

Q W E R T Y U I O P
A S D F G H J K L
Z X C V B N M

Clue: containers

MEDIUM

Puzzle 105

MEDIUM

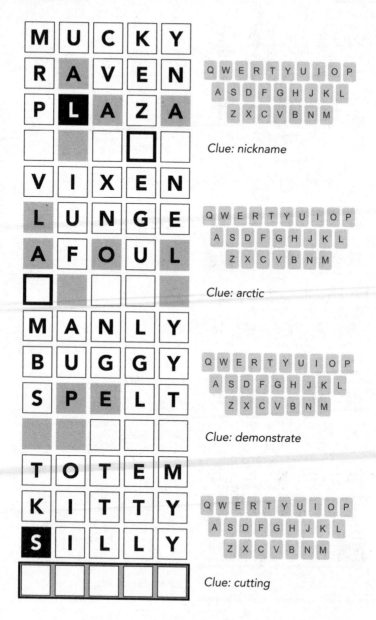

M	U	C	K	Y	
R	A	V	E	N	Q W E R T Y U I O P / A S D F G H J K L / Z X C V B N M
P	L	A	Z	A	
					Clue: nickname
V	I	X	E	N	
L	U	N	G	E	Q W E R T Y U I O P / A S D F G H J K L / Z X C V B N M
A	F	O	U	L	
					Clue: arctic
M	A	N	L	Y	
B	U	G	G	Y	Q W E R T Y U I O P / A S D F G H J K L / Z X C V B N M
S	P	E	L	T	
					Clue: demonstrate
T	O	T	E	M	
K	I	T	T	Y	Q W E R T Y U I O P / A S D F G H J K L / Z X C V B N M
S	I	L	L	Y	
					Clue: cutting

Puzzle 106

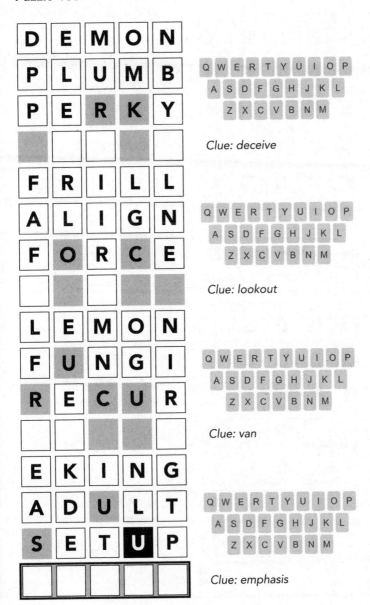

D	E	M	O	N
P	L	U	M	B
P	E	R	K	Y
F	R	I	L	L
A	L	I	G	N
F	O	R	C	E
L	E	M	O	N
F	U	N	G	I
R	E	C	U	R
E	K	I	N	G
A	D	U	L	T
S	E	T	U	P

Q W E R T Y U I O P
A S D F G H J K L
Z X C V B N M

Clue: deceive

Q W E R T Y U I O P
A S D F G H J K L
Z X C V B N M

Clue: lookout

Q W E R T Y U I O P
A S D F G H J K L
Z X C V B N M

Clue: van

Q W E R T Y U I O P
A S D F G H J K L
Z X C V B N M

Clue: emphasis

Puzzle 107

MEDIUM

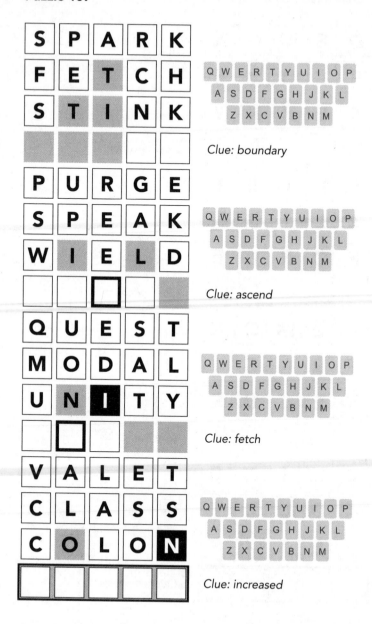

S	P	A	R	K
F	E	T	C	H
S	T	I	N	K

Q W E R T Y U I O P
A S D F G H J K L
Z X C V B N M

Clue: boundary

P	U	R	G	E
S	P	E	A	K
W	I	E	L	D

Q W E R T Y U I O P
A S D F G H J K L
Z X C V B N M

Clue: ascend

Q	U	E	S	T
M	O	D	A	L
U	N	I	T	Y

Q W E R T Y U I O P
A S D F G H J K L
Z X C V B N M

Clue: fetch

V	A	L	E	T
C	L	A	S	S
C	O	L	O	N

Q W E R T Y U I O P
A S D F G H J K L
Z X C V B N M

Clue: increased

Puzzle 108

C	H	A	F	F
B	E	F	I	T
E	N	E	M	Y
S	L	Y	L	Y
M	U	R	K	Y
T	U	R	B	O
C	L	A	C	K
P	A	R	R	Y
P	U	F	F	Y
S	L	E	E	P
D	U	S	K	Y
G	U	E	S	S

Q W E R T Y U I O P
A S D F G H J K L
Z X C V B N M

Clue: matter

Q W E R T Y U I O P
A S D F G H J K L
Z X C V B N M

Clue: completely

Q W E R T Y U I O P
A S D F G H J K L
Z X C V B N M

Clue: direction

Q W E R T Y U I O P
A S D F G H J K L
Z X C V B N M

Clue: money

MEDIUM

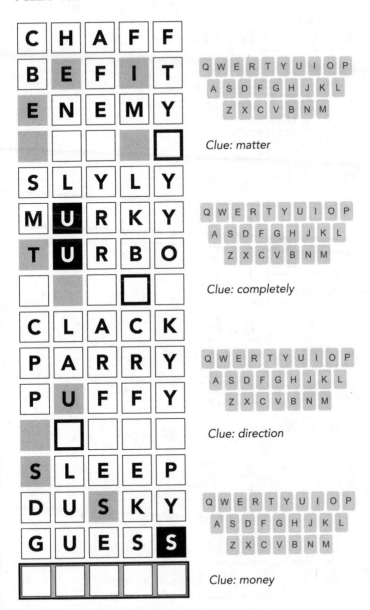

MEDIUM

Puzzle 109

L	Y	I	N	G
D	R	O	W	N
T	E	A	C	H

Q W E R T Y U I O P
A S D F G H J K L
Z X C V B N M

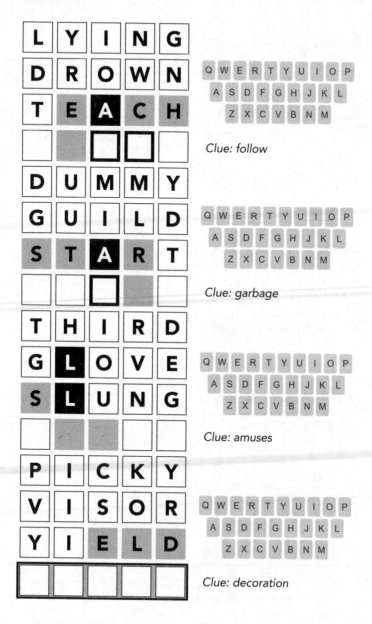

Clue: follow

D	U	M	M	Y
G	U	I	L	D
S	T	A	R	T

Q W E R T Y U I O P
A S D F G H J K L
Z X C V B N M

Clue: garbage

T	H	I	R	D
G	L	O	V	E
S	L	U	N	G

Q W E R T Y U I O P
A S D F G H J K L
Z X C V B N M

Clue: amuses

P	I	C	K	Y
V	I	S	O	R
Y	I	E	L	D

Q W E R T Y U I O P
A S D F G H J K L
Z X C V B N M

Clue: decoration

Puzzle 110

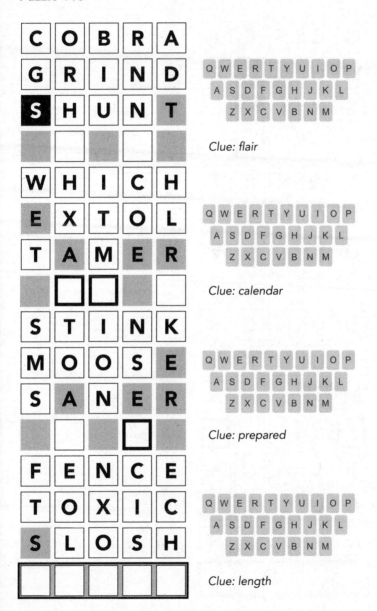

C	O	B	R	A
G	R	I	N	D
S	H	U	N	T
W	H	I	C	H
E	X	T	O	L
T	A	M	E	R
S	T	I	N	K
M	O	O	S	E
S	A	N	E	R
F	E	N	C	E
T	O	X	I	C
S	L	O	S	H

Q W E R T Y U I O P
A S D F G H J K L
Z X C V B N M

Clue: flair

Q W E R T Y U I O P
A S D F G H J K L
Z X C V B N M

Clue: calendar

Q W E R T Y U I O P
A S D F G H J K L
Z X C V B N M

Clue: prepared

Q W E R T Y U I O P
A S D F G H J K L
Z X C V B N M

Clue: length

MEDIUM

Puzzle 111

MEDIUM

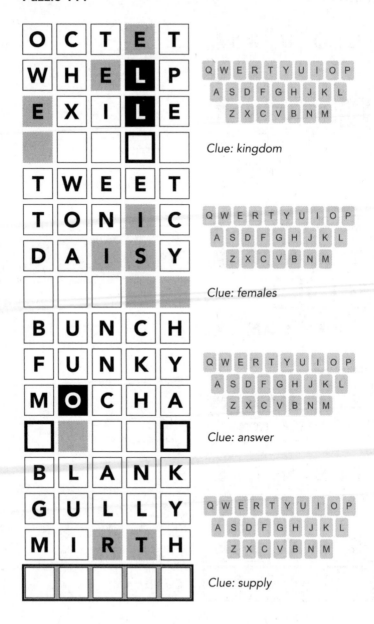

O	C	T	E	T	
W	H	E	L	P	Q W E R T Y U I O P A S D F G H J K L Z X C V B N M
E	X	I	L	E	
					Clue: kingdom
T	W	E	E	T	
T	O	N	I	C	Q W E R T Y U I O P A S D F G H J K L Z X C V B N M
D	A	I	S	Y	
					Clue: females
B	U	N	C	H	
F	U	N	K	Y	Q W E R T Y U I O P A S D F G H J K L Z X C V B N M
M	O	C	H	A	
					Clue: answer
B	L	A	N	K	
G	U	L	L	Y	Q W E R T Y U I O P A S D F G H J K L Z X C V B N M
M	I	R	T	H	
					Clue: supply

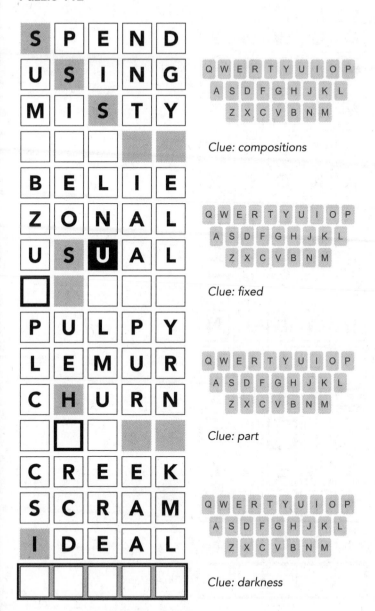

Puzzle 112

S	P	E	N	D
U	S	I	N	G
M	I	S	T	Y
B	E	L	I	E
Z	O	N	A	L
U	S	U	A	L
P	U	L	P	Y
L	E	M	U	R
C	H	U	R	N
C	R	E	E	K
S	C	R	A	M
I	D	E	A	L

Q W E R T Y U I O P
A S D F G H J K L
Z X C V B N M

Clue: compositions

Q W E R T Y U I O P
A S D F G H J K L
Z X C V B N M

Clue: fixed

Q W E R T Y U I O P
A S D F G H J K L
Z X C V B N M

Clue: part

Q W E R T Y U I O P
A S D F G H J K L
Z X C V B N M

Clue: darkness

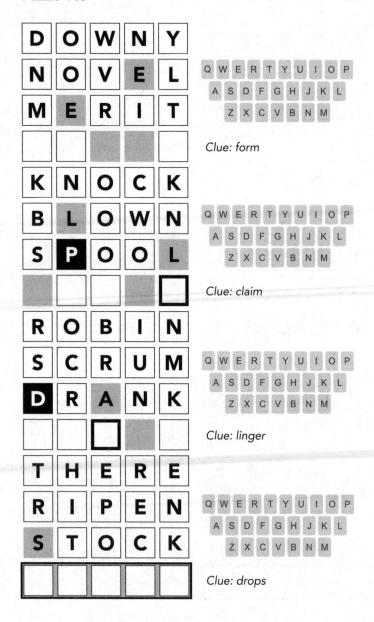

MEDIUM

Puzzle 113

D	O	W	N	Y	
N	O	V	E	L	QWERTYUIOP / ASDFGHJKL / ZXCVBNM
M	E	R	I	T	
					Clue: form
K	N	O	C	K	
B	L	O	W	N	QWERTYUIOP / ASDFGHJKL / ZXCVBNM
S	P	O	O	L	
					Clue: claim
R	O	B	I	N	
S	C	R	U	M	QWERTYUIOP / ASDFGHJKL / ZXCVBNM
D	R	A	N	K	
					Clue: linger
T	H	E	R	E	
R	I	P	E	N	QWERTYUIOP / ASDFGHJKL / ZXCVBNM
S	T	O	C	K	
					Clue: drops

Puzzle 114

B	L	O	O	M
W	I	S	E	R
S	I	R	E	N

Q W E R T Y U I O P
A S D F G H J K L
Z X C V B N M

Clue: royalty

B	E	Z	E	L
S	P	O	K	E
T	H	R	O	B

Q W E R T Y U I O P
A S D F G H J K L
Z X C V B N M

Clue: shackles

S	C	R	U	M
B	R	O	O	D
R	E	A	R	M

Q W E R T Y U I O P
A S D F G H J K L
Z X C V B N M

Clue: sprite

D	O	N	O	R
C	O	U	L	D
T	R	I	T	E

Q W E R T Y U I O P
A S D F G H J K L
Z X C V B N M

Clue: perhaps

MEDIUM

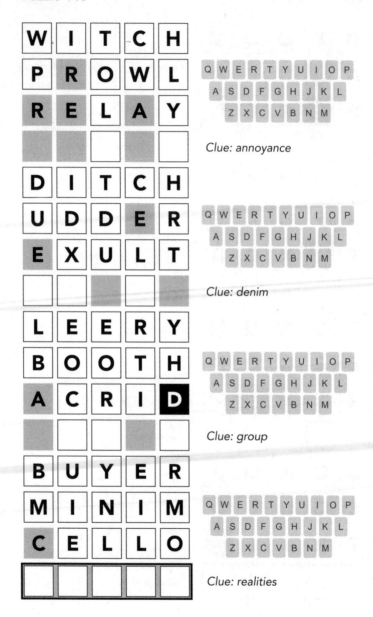

MEDIUM

Puzzle 115

W	I	T	C	H
P	R	O	W	L
R	E	L	A	Y

Q W E R T Y U I O P
A S D F G H J K L
Z X C V B N M

Clue: annoyance

D	I	T	C	H
U	D	D	E	R
E	X	U	L	T

Q W E R T Y U I O P
A S D F G H J K L
Z X C V B N M

Clue: denim

L	E	E	R	Y
B	O	O	T	H
A	C	R	I	D

Q W E R T Y U I O P
A S D F G H J K L
Z X C V B N M

Clue: group

B	U	Y	E	R
M	I	N	I	M
C	E	L	L	O

Q W E R T Y U I O P
A S D F G H J K L
Z X C V B N M

Clue: realities

Puzzle 116

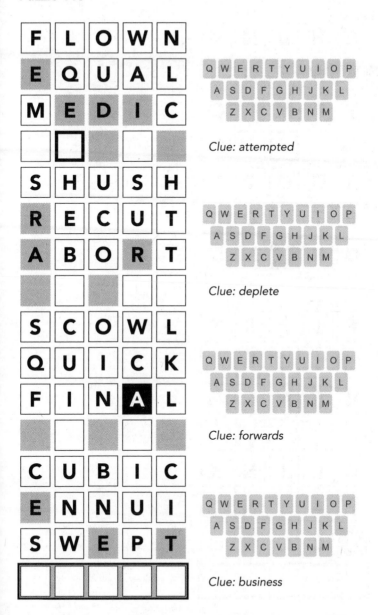

F	L	O	W	N
E	Q	U	A	L
M	E	D	I	C
S	H	U	S	H
R	E	C	U	T
A	B	O	R	T
S	C	O	W	L
Q	U	I	C	K
F	I	N	A	L
C	U	B	I	C
E	N	N	U	I
S	W	E	P	T

Q W E R T Y U I O P
A S D F G H J K L
Z X C V B N M

Clue: attempted

Q W E R T Y U I O P
A S D F G H J K L
Z X C V B N M

Clue: deplete

Q W E R T Y U I O P
A S D F G H J K L
Z X C V B N M

Clue: forwards

Q W E R T Y U I O P
A S D F G H J K L
Z X C V B N M

Clue: business

Puzzle 117

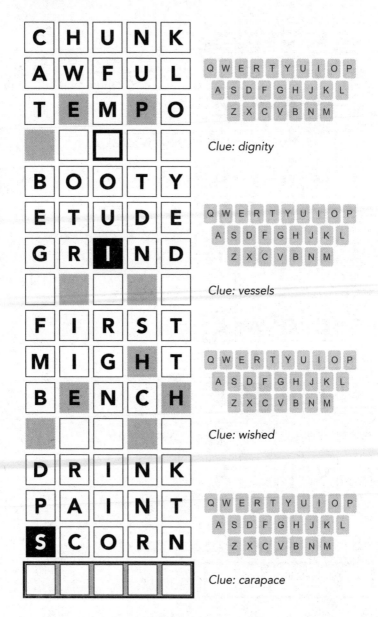

MEDIUM

C	H	U	N	K
A	W	F	U	L
T	E	M	P	O

Q W E R T Y U I O P
A S D F G H J K L
Z X C V B N M

Clue: dignity

B	O	O	T	Y
E	T	U	D	E
G	R	I	N	D

Q W E R T Y U I O P
A S D F G H J K L
Z X C V B N M

Clue: vessels

F	I	R	S	T
M	I	G	H	T
B	E	N	C	H

Q W E R T Y U I O P
A S D F G H J K L
Z X C V B N M

Clue: wished

D	R	I	N	K
P	A	I	N	T
S	C	O	R	N

Q W E R T Y U I O P
A S D F G H J K L
Z X C V B N M

Clue: carapace

Puzzle 118

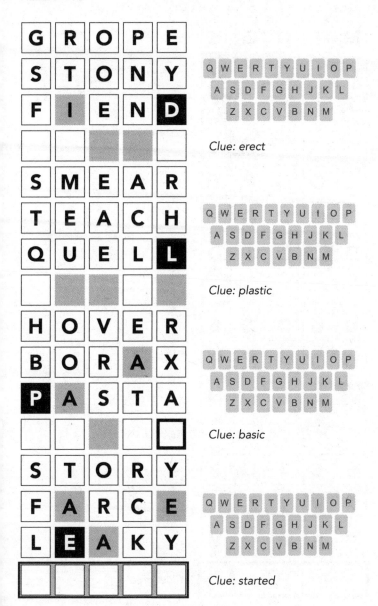

G	R	O	P	E
S	T	O	N	Y
F	I	E	N	D

Q W E R T Y U I O P
A S D F G H J K L
Z X C V B N M

Clue: erect

S	M	E	A	R
T	E	A	C	H
Q	U	E	L	L

Q W E R T Y U I O P
A S D F G H J K L
Z X C V B N M

Clue: plastic

H	O	V	E	R
B	O	R	A	X
P	A	S	T	A

Q W E R T Y U I O P
A S D F G H J K L
Z X C V B N M

Clue: basic

S	T	O	R	Y
F	A	R	C	E
L	E	A	K	Y

Q W E R T Y U I O P
A S D F G H J K L
Z X C V B N M

Clue: started

MEDIUM

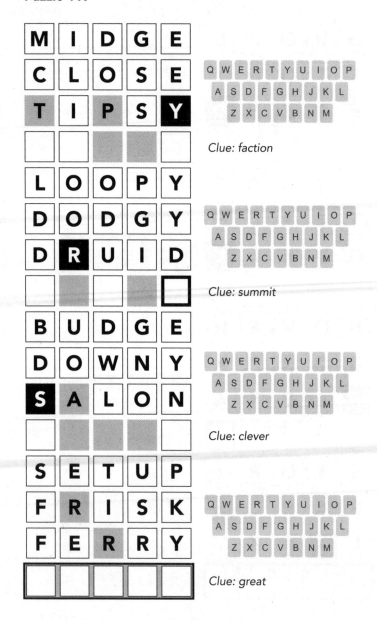

MEDIUM

Puzzle 119

M	I	D	G	E
C	L	O	S	E
T	I	P	S	Y

Q W E R T Y U I O P
A S D F G H J K L
Z X C V B N M

Clue: faction

L	O	O	P	Y
D	O	D	G	Y
D	R	U	I	D

Q W E R T Y U I O P
A S D F G H J K L
Z X C V B N M

Clue: summit

B	U	D	G	E
D	O	W	N	Y
S	A	L	O	N

Q W E R T Y U I O P
A S D F G H J K L
Z X C V B N M

Clue: clever

S	E	T	U	P
F	R	I	S	K
F	E	R	R	Y

Q W E R T Y U I O P
A S D F G H J K L
Z X C V B N M

Clue: great

Puzzle 120

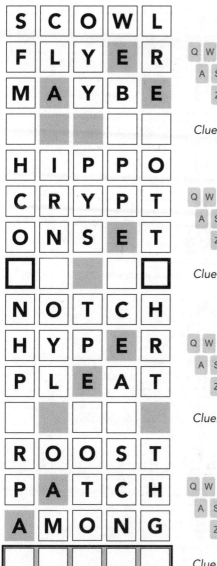

S	C	O	W	L
F	L	Y	E	R
M	A	Y	B	E

Q W E R T Y U I O P
A S D F G H J K L
Z X C V B N M

Clue: demise

H	I	P	P	O
C	R	Y	P	T
O	N	S	E	T

Q W E R T Y U I O P
A S D F G H J K L
Z X C V B N M

Clue: measure

N	O	T	C	H
H	Y	P	E	R
P	L	E	A	T

Q W E R T Y U I O P
A S D F G H J K L
Z X C V B N M

Clue: escort

R	O	O	S	T
P	A	T	C	H
A	M	O	N	G

Q W E R T Y U I O P
A S D F G H J K L
Z X C V B N M

Clue: fair

MEDIUM

Puzzle 121

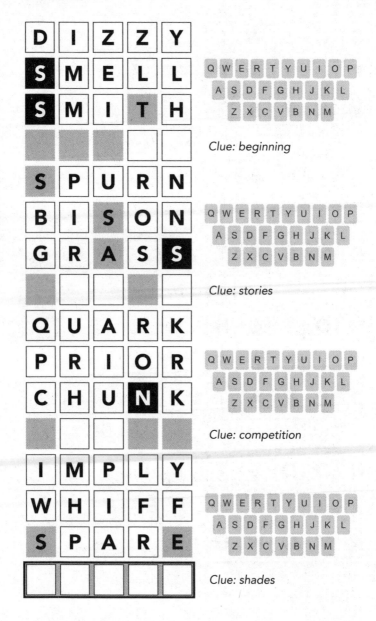

MEDIUM

D	I	Z	Z	Y
S	M	E	L	L
S	M	I	T	H

QWERTYUIOP
ASDFGHJKL
ZXCVBNM

Clue: beginning

S	P	U	R	N
B	I	S	O	N
G	R	A	S	S

QWERTYUIOP
ASDFGHJKL
ZXCVBNM

Clue: stories

Q	U	A	R	K
P	R	I	O	R
C	H	U	N	K

QWERTYUIOP
ASDFGHJKL
ZXCVBNM

Clue: competition

I	M	P	L	Y
W	H	I	F	F
S	P	A	R	E

QWERTYUIOP
ASDFGHJKL
ZXCVBNM

Clue: shades

Puzzle 122

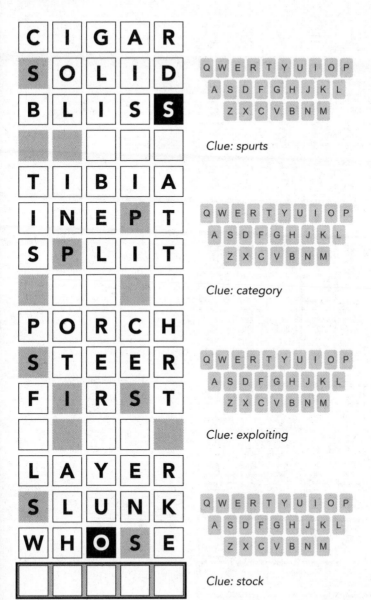

C	I	G	A	R
S	O	L	I	D
B	L	I	S	S

Q W E R T Y U I O P
A S D F G H J K L
Z X C V B N M

Clue: spurts

T	I	B	I	A
I	N	E	P	T
S	P	L	I	T

Q W E R T Y U I O P
A S D F G H J K L
Z X C V B N M

Clue: category

P	O	R	C	H
S	T	E	E	R
F	I	R	S	T

Q W E R T Y U I O P
A S D F G H J K L
Z X C V B N M

Clue: exploiting

L	A	Y	E	R
S	L	U	N	K
W	H	O	S	E

Q W E R T Y U I O P
A S D F G H J K L
Z X C V B N M

Clue: stock

MEDIUM

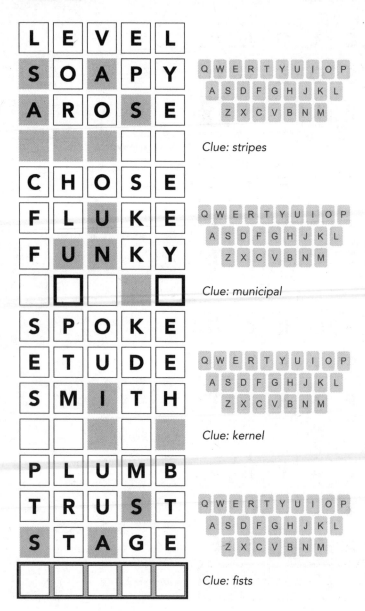

Puzzle 123

L	E	V	E	L	
S	O	A	P	Y	Q W E R T Y U I O P
A	R	O	S	E	A S D F G H J K L Z X C V B N M
					Clue: stripes
C	H	O	S	E	
F	L	U	K	E	Q W E R T Y U I O P
F	U	N	K	Y	A S D F G H J K L Z X C V B N M
					Clue: municipal
S	P	O	K	E	
E	T	U	D	E	Q W E R T Y U I O P
S	M	I	T	H	A S D F G H J K L Z X C V B N M
					Clue: kernel
P	L	U	M	B	
T	R	U	S	T	Q W E R T Y U I O P
S	T	A	G	E	A S D F G H J K L Z X C V B N M
					Clue: fists

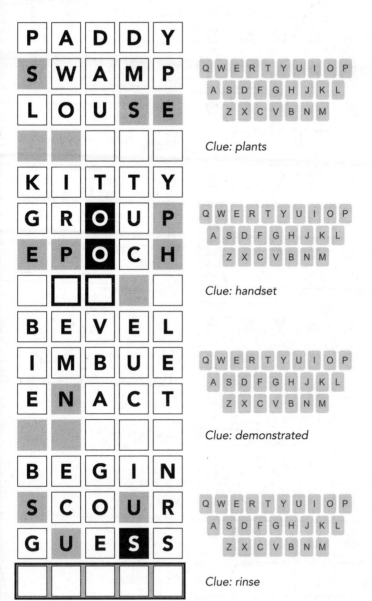

Puzzle 124

P	A	D	D	Y
S	W	A	M	P
L	O	U	S	E

Q W E R T Y U I O P
A S D F G H J K L
Z X C V B N M

Clue: plants

K	I	T	T	Y
G	R	O	U	P
E	P	O	C	H

Q W E R T Y U I O P
A S D F G H J K L
Z X C V B N M

Clue: handset

B	E	V	E	L
I	M	B	U	E
E	N	A	C	T

Q W E R T Y U I O P
A S D F G H J K L
Z X C V B N M

Clue: demonstrated

B	E	G	I	N
S	C	O	U	R
G	U	E	S	S

Q W E R T Y U I O P
A S D F G H J K L
Z X C V B N M

Clue: rinse

MEDIUM

Puzzle 125

C	R	U	M	B
G	R	A	Z	E
S	A	W	E	D

QWERTYUIOP
ASDFGHJKL
ZXCVBNM

Clue: fly

D	R	E	S	S
O	N	S	E	T
O	C	T	E	T

QWERTYUIOP
ASDFGHJKL
ZXCVBNM

Clue: clenched

R	H	Y	M	E
D	E	L	V	E
S	N	A	R	E

QWERTYUIOP
ASDFGHJKL
ZXCVBNM

Clue: indicate

J	U	M	B	O
B	U	L	K	Y
A	U	D	I	T

QWERTYUIOP
ASDFGHJKL
ZXCVBNM

Clue: instruct

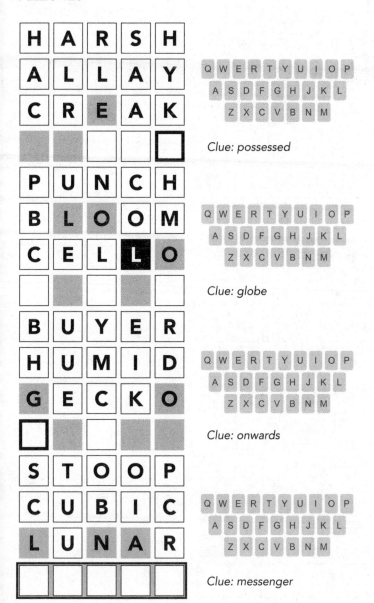

Puzzle 126

H	A	R	S	H
A	L	L	A	Y
C	R	E	A	K

Q W E R T Y U I O P
A S D F G H J K L
Z X C V B N M

Clue: possessed

P	U	N	C	H
B	L	O	O	M
C	E	L	L	O

Q W E R T Y U I O P
A S D F G H J K L
Z X C V B N M

Clue: globe

B	U	Y	E	R
H	U	M	I	D
G	E	C	K	O

Q W E R T Y U I O P
A S D F G H J K L
Z X C V B N M

Clue: onwards

S	T	O	O	P
C	U	B	I	C
L	U	N	A	R

Q W E R T Y U I O P
A S D F G H J K L
Z X C V B N M

Clue: messenger

MEDIUM

Puzzle 127

MEDIUM

T	O	R	C	H
G	R	O	S	S
W	E	A	R	Y

Q W E R T Y U I O P
A S D F G H J K L
Z X C V B N M

Clue: responsibility

L	I	M	B	O
C	Y	N	I	C
S	A	T	I	N

Q W E R T Y U I O P
A S D F G H J K L
Z X C V B N M

Clue: pay

S	Y	R	U	P
C	L	U	M	P
S	W	I	R	L

Q W E R T Y U I O P
A S D F G H J K L
Z X C V B N M

Clue: beneath

D	O	U	G	H
C	A	N	O	E
A	D	O	B	E

Q W E R T Y U I O P
A S D F G H J K L
Z X C V B N M

Clue: dish

Puzzle 128

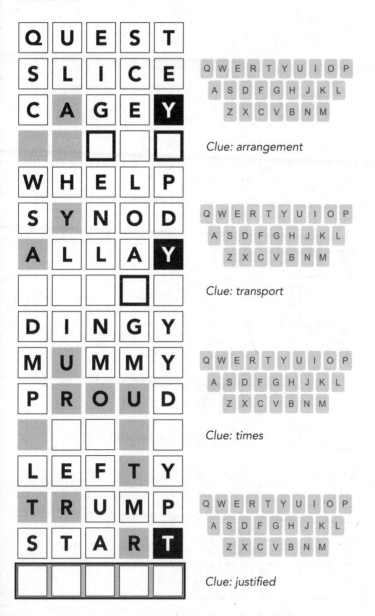

Q	U	E	S	T
S	L	I	C	E
C	A	G	E	Y
W	H	E	L	P
S	Y	N	O	D
A	L	L	A	Y
D	I	N	G	Y
M	U	M	M	Y
P	R	O	U	D
L	E	F	T	Y
T	R	U	M	P
S	T	A	R	T

Q W E R T Y U I O P
A S D F G H J K L
Z X C V B N M

Clue: arrangement

Q W E R T Y U I O P
A S D F G H J K L
Z X C V B N M

Clue: transport

Q W E R T Y U I O P
A S D F G H J K L
Z X C V B N M

Clue: times

Q W E R T Y U I O P
A S D F G H J K L
Z X C V B N M

Clue: justified

Puzzle 129

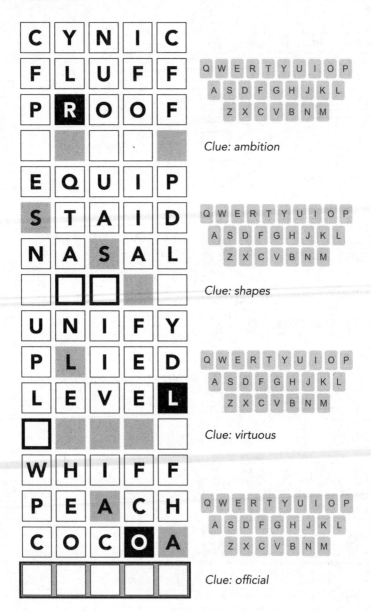

MEDIUM

C	Y	N	I	C
F	L	U	F	F
P	R	O	O	F

Q W E R T Y U I O P
A S D F G H J K L
Z X C V B N M

Clue: ambition

E	Q	U	I	P
S	T	A	I	D
N	A	S	A	L

Q W E R T Y U I O P
A S D F G H J K L
Z X C V B N M

Clue: shapes

U	N	I	F	Y
P	L	I	E	D
L	E	V	E	L

Q W E R T Y U I O P
A S D F G H J K L
Z X C V B N M

Clue: virtuous

W	H	I	F	F
P	E	A	C	H
C	O	C	O	A

Q W E R T Y U I O P
A S D F G H J K L
Z X C V B N M

Clue: official

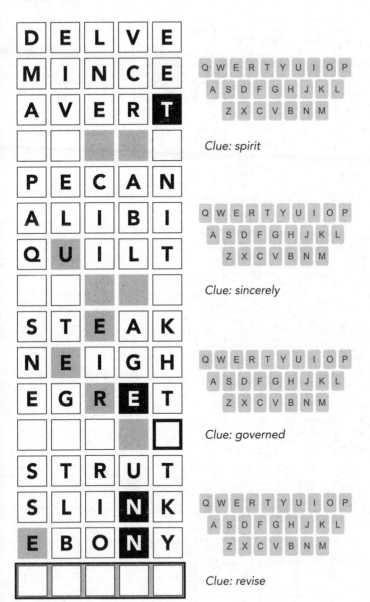

Puzzle 130

D	E	L	V	E
M	I	N	C	E
A	V	E	R	T

Q W E R T Y U I O P
A S D F G H J K L
Z X C V B N M

Clue: spirit

P	E	C	A	N
A	L	I	B	I
Q	U	I	L	T

Q W E R T Y U I O P
A S D F G H J K L
Z X C V B N M

Clue: sincerely

S	T	E	A	K
N	E	I	G	H
E	G	R	E	T

Q W E R T Y U I O P
A S D F G H J K L
Z X C V B N M

Clue: governed

S	T	R	U	T
S	L	I	N	K
E	B	O	N	Y

Q W E R T Y U I O P
A S D F G H J K L
Z X C V B N M

Clue: revise

MEDIUM

MEDIUM

Puzzle 131

F	U	N	N	Y	
A	R	E	N	A	Q W E R T Y U I O P A S D F G H J K L Z X C V B N M
C	R	O	S	S	
					Clue: offspring
M	O	N	T	H	
B	R	U	N	T	Q W E R T Y U I O P A S D F G H J K L Z X C V B N M
V	I	L	L	A	
					Clue: circles
W	A	G	O	N	
S	W	E	A	R	Q W E R T Y U I O P A S D F G H J K L Z X C V B N M
J	O	I	S	T	
					Clue: harvests
O	F	F	A	L	
W	O	M	E	N	Q W E R T Y U I O P A S D F G H J K L Z X C V B N M
B	L	E	E	D	
					Clue: cost

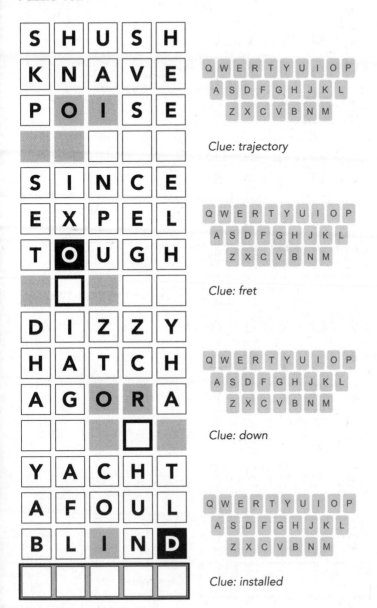

Puzzle 132

S	H	U	S	H
K	N	A	V	E
P	O	I	S	E
S	I	N	C	E
E	X	P	E	L
T	O	U	G	H
D	I	Z	Z	Y
H	A	T	C	H
A	G	O	R	A
Y	A	C	H	T
A	F	O	U	L
B	L	I	N	D

Q W E R T Y U I O P
A S D F G H J K L
Z X C V B N M

Clue: trajectory

Q W E R T Y U I O P
A S D F G H J K L
Z X C V B N M

Clue: fret

Q W E R T Y U I O P
A S D F G H J K L
Z X C V B N M

Clue: down

Q W E R T Y U I O P
A S D F G H J K L
Z X C V B N M

Clue: installed

MEDIUM

Puzzle 133

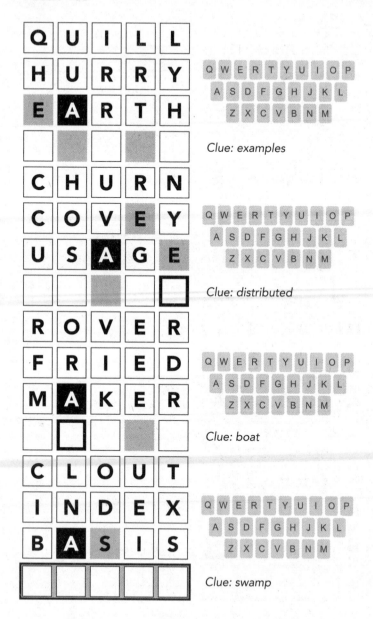

MEDIUM

Q	U	I	L	L	
H	U	R	R	Y	Q W E R T Y U I O P A S D F G H J K L Z X C V B N M
E	A	R	T	H	
					Clue: examples
C	H	U	R	N	
C	O	V	E	Y	Q W E R T Y U I O P A S D F G H J K L Z X C V B N M
U	S	A	G	E	
					Clue: distributed
R	O	V	E	R	
F	R	I	E	D	Q W E R T Y U I O P A S D F G H J K L Z X C V B N M
M	A	K	E	R	
					Clue: boat
C	L	O	U	T	
I	N	D	E	X	Q W E R T Y U I O P A S D F G H J K L Z X C V B N M
B	A	S	I	S	
					Clue: swamp

Puzzle 134

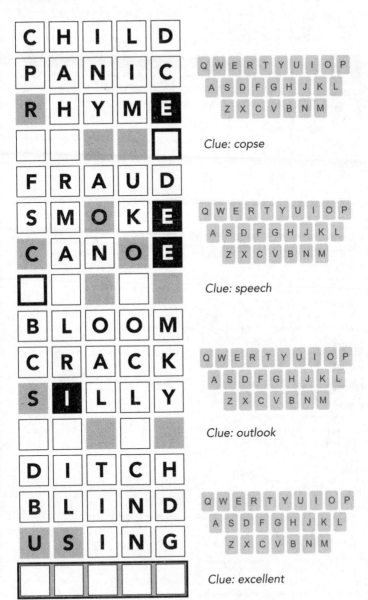

C	H	I	L	D
P	A	N	I	C
R	H	Y	M	E

Q W E R T Y U I O P
A S D F G H J K L
Z X C V B N M

Clue: copse

F	R	A	U	D
S	M	O	K	E
C	A	N	O	E

Q W E R T Y U I O P
A S D F G H J K L
Z X C V B N M

Clue: speech

B	L	O	O	M
C	R	A	C	K
S	I	L	L	Y

Q W E R T Y U I O P
A S D F G H J K L
Z X C V B N M

Clue: outlook

D	I	T	C	H
B	L	I	N	D
U	S	I	N	G

Q W E R T Y U I O P
A S D F G H J K L
Z X C V B N M

Clue: excellent

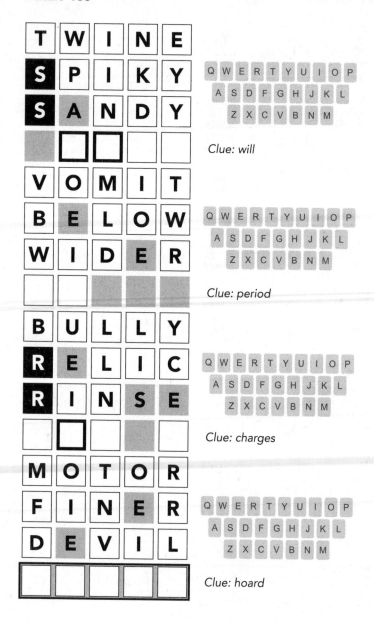

Puzzle 135

MEDIUM

T	W	I	N	E	
S	P	I	K	Y	QWERTYUIOP ASDFGHJKL ZXCVBNM
S	A	N	D	Y	
					Clue: will
V	O	M	I	T	
B	E	L	O	W	QWERTYUIOP ASDFGHJKL ZXCVBNM
W	I	D	E	R	
					Clue: period
B	U	L	L	Y	
R	E	L	I	C	QWERTYUIOP ASDFGHJKL ZXCVBNM
R	I	N	S	E	
					Clue: charges
M	O	T	O	R	
F	I	N	E	R	QWERTYUIOP ASDFGHJKL ZXCVBNM
D	E	V	I	L	
					Clue: hoard

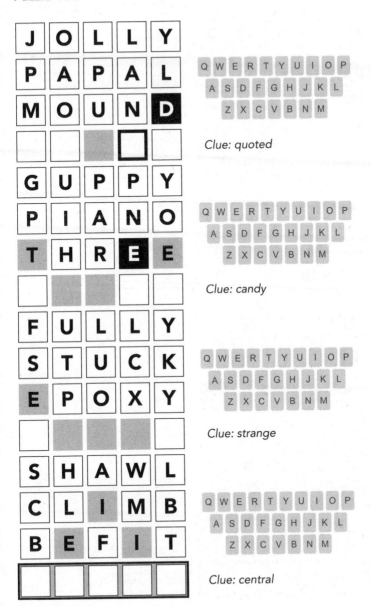

Puzzle 136

J	O	L	L	Y
P	A	P	A	L
M	O	U	N	D

Q W E R T Y U I O P
A S D F G H J K L
Z X C V B N M

Clue: quoted

G	U	P	P	Y
P	I	A	N	O
T	H	R	E	E

Q W E R T Y U I O P
A S D F G H J K L
Z X C V B N M

Clue: candy

F	U	L	L	Y
S	T	U	C	K
E	P	O	X	Y

Q W E R T Y U I O P
A S D F G H J K L
Z X C V B N M

Clue: strange

S	H	A	W	L
C	L	I	M	B
B	E	F	I	T

Q W E R T Y U I O P
A S D F G H J K L
Z X C V B N M

Clue: central

MEDIUM

Puzzle 137

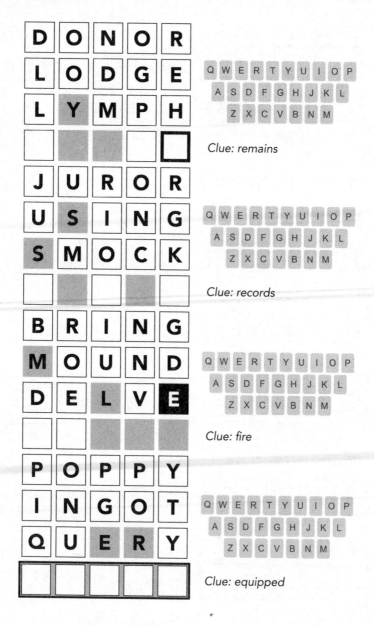

MEDIUM

D	O	N	O	R
L	O	D	G	E
L	Y	M	P	H

Q W E R T Y U I O P
A S D F G H J K L
Z X C V B N M

Clue: remains

J	U	R	O	R
U	S	I	N	G
S	M	O	C	K

Q W E R T Y U I O P
A S D F G H J K L
Z X C V B N M

Clue: records

B	R	I	N	G
M	O	U	N	D
D	E	L	V	E

Q W E R T Y U I O P
A S D F G H J K L
Z X C V B N M

Clue: fire

P	O	P	P	Y
I	N	G	O	T
Q	U	E	R	Y

Q W E R T Y U I O P
A S D F G H J K L
Z X C V B N M

Clue: equipped

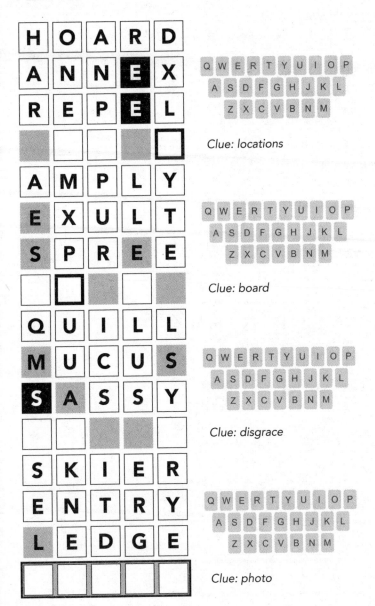

Puzzle 138

H	O	A	R	D	
A	N	N	E	X	
R	E	P	E	L	
					Clue: *locations*
A	M	P	L	Y	
E	X	U	L	T	
S	P	R	E	E	
					Clue: *board*
Q	U	I	L	L	
M	U	C	U	S	
S	A	S	S	Y	
					Clue: *disgrace*
S	K	I	E	R	
E	N	T	R	Y	
L	E	D	G	E	
					Clue: *photo*

Q W E R T Y U I O P
A S D F G H J K L
Z X C V B N M

Clue: *locations*

Q W E R T Y U I O P
A S D F G H J K L
Z X C V B N M

Clue: *board*

Q W E R T Y U I O P
A S D F G H J K L
Z X C V B N M

Clue: *disgrace*

Q W E R T Y U I O P
A S D F G H J K L
Z X C V B N M

Clue: *photo*

Puzzle 139

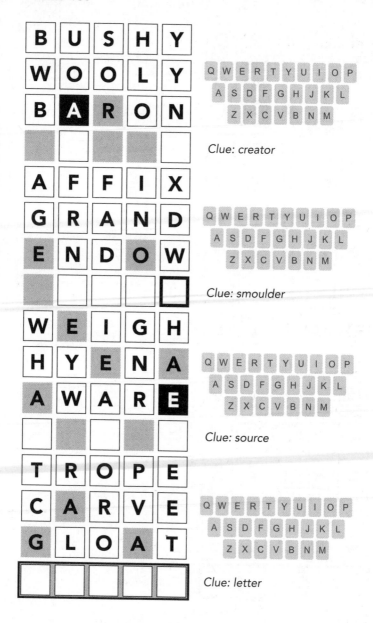

MEDIUM

B	U	S	H	Y
W	O	O	L	Y
B	A	R	O	N

Q W E R T Y U I O P
A S D F G H J K L
Z X C V B N M

Clue: creator

A	F	F	I	X
G	R	A	N	D
E	N	D	O	W

Q W E R T Y U I O P
A S D F G H J K L
Z X C V B N M

Clue: smoulder

W	E	I	G	H
H	Y	E	N	A
A	W	A	R	E

Q W E R T Y U I O P
A S D F G H J K L
Z X C V B N M

Clue: source

T	R	O	P	E
C	A	R	V	E
G	L	O	A	T

Q W E R T Y U I O P
A S D F G H J K L
Z X C V B N M

Clue: letter

Puzzle 140

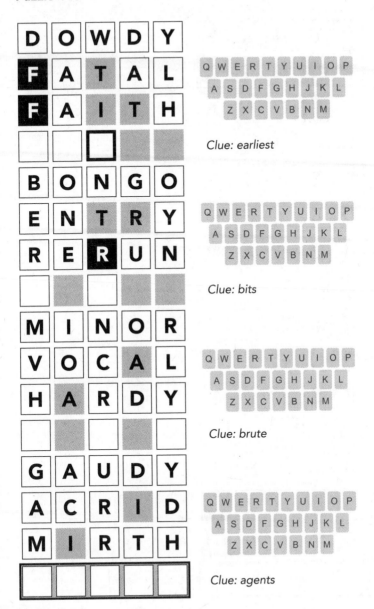

D	O	W	D	Y
F	A	T	A	L
F	A	I	T	H

Q W E R T Y U I O P
A S D F G H J K L
Z X C V B N M

Clue: earliest

B	O	N	G	O
E	N	T	R	Y
R	E	R	U	N

Q W E R T Y U I O P
A S D F G H J K L
Z X C V B N M

Clue: bits

M	I	N	O	R
V	O	C	A	L
H	A	R	D	Y

Q W E R T Y U I O P
A S D F G H J K L
Z X C V B N M

Clue: brute

G	A	U	D	Y
A	C	R	I	D
M	I	R	T	H

Q W E R T Y U I O P
A S D F G H J K L
Z X C V B N M

Clue: agents

MEDIUM

Puzzle 141

MEDIUM

P	E	R	K	Y
P	A	N	I	C
F	A	U	N	A

Q W E R T Y U I O P
A S D F G H J K L
Z X C V B N M

Clue: stone worker

F	L	A	I	R
D	R	Y	E	R
B	E	G	A	N

Q W E R T Y U I O P
A S D F G H J K L
Z X C V B N M

Clue: rhymes

E	A	R	L	Y
Q	U	E	L	L
R	E	S	E	T

Q W E R T Y U I O P
A S D F G H J K L
Z X C V B N M

Clue: stated

G	I	A	N	T
G	L	A	Z	E
S	T	A	L	E

Q W E R T Y U I O P
A S D F G H J K L
Z X C V B N M

Clue: insecure

Puzzle 142

M	E	R	I	T
B	R	A	S	S
R	E	F	E	R

Q W E R T Y U I O P
A S D F G H J K L
Z X C V B N M

Clue: ground

F	A	I	N	T
T	R	U	M	P
B	A	L	E	R

Q W E R T Y U I O P
A S D F G H J K L
Z X C V B N M

Clue: substandard

F	L	O	C	K
H	U	N	K	Y
T	R	Y	S	T

Q W E R T Y U I O P
A S D F G H J K L
Z X C V B N M

Clue: spouses

D	U	M	M	Y
T	O	U	C	H
S	C	O	P	E

Q W E R T Y U I O P
A S D F G H J K L
Z X C V B N M

Clue: tomb

MEDIUM

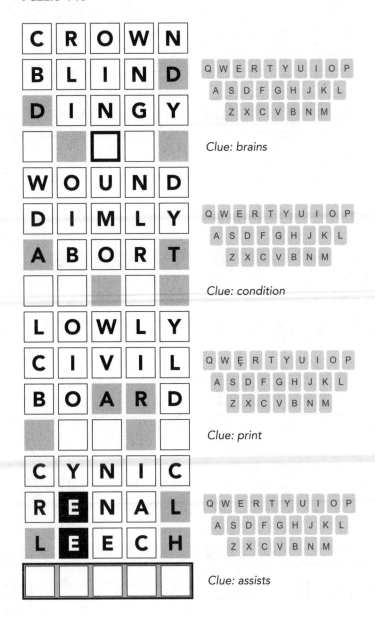

MEDIUM

Puzzle 143

C R O W N
B L I N D
D I N G Y

Q W E R T Y U I O P
A S D F G H J K L
Z X C V B N M

Clue: brains

W O U N D
D I M L Y
A B O R T

Q W E R T Y U I O P
A S D F G H J K L
Z X C V B N M

Clue: condition

L O W L Y
C I V I L
B O A R D

Q W E R T Y U I O P
A S D F G H J K L
Z X C V B N M

Clue: print

C Y N I C
R E N A L
L E E C H

Q W E R T Y U I O P
A S D F G H J K L
Z X C V B N M

Clue: assists

Puzzle 144

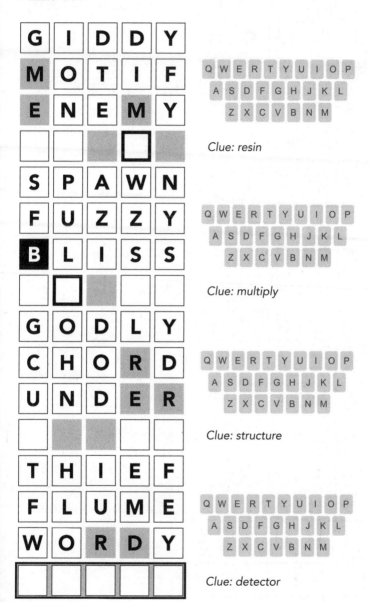

G	I	D	D	Y
M	O	T	I	F
E	N	E	M	Y

Q W E R T Y U I O P
A S D F G H J K L
Z X C V B N M

Clue: resin

S	P	A	W	N
F	U	Z	Z	Y
B	L	I	S	S

Q W E R T Y U I O P
A S D F G H J K L
Z X C V B N M

Clue: multiply

G	O	D	L	Y
C	H	O	R	D
U	N	D	E	R

Q W E R T Y U I O P
A S D F G H J K L
Z X C V B N M

Clue: structure

T	H	I	E	F
F	L	U	M	E
W	O	R	D	Y

Q W E R T Y U I O P
A S D F G H J K L
Z X C V B N M

Clue: detector

MEDIUM

MEDIUM

Puzzle 145

H	I	T	C	H
L	U	C	I	D
S	P	I	L	T

QWERTYUIOP
ASDFGHJKL
ZXCVBNM

Clue: necklace

R	E	F	I	T
G	L	E	A	N
E	A	G	L	E

QWERTYUIOP
ASDFGHJKL
ZXCVBNM

Clue: pools

M	I	N	T	Y
R	E	B	U	S
A	W	A	K	E

QWERTYUIOP
ASDFGHJKL
ZXCVBNM

Clue: examine

C	O	Y	L	Y
S	H	A	L	L
B	R	U	T	E

QWERTYUIOP
ASDFGHJKL
ZXCVBNM

Clue: cut

Puzzle 146

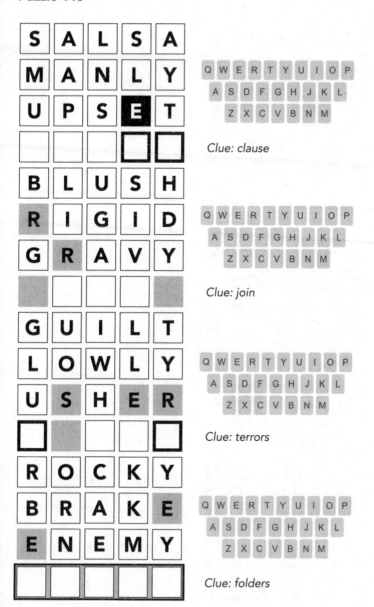

S	A	L	S	A
M	A	N	L	Y
U	P	S	E	T

Q W E R T Y U I O P
A S D F G H J K L
Z X C V B N M

Clue: clause

B	L	U	S	H
R	I	G	I	D
G	R	A	V	Y

Q W E R T Y U I O P
A S D F G H J K L
Z X C V B N M

Clue: join

G	U	I	L	T
L	O	W	L	Y
U	S	H	E	R

Q W E R T Y U I O P
A S D F G H J K L
Z X C V B N M

Clue: terrors

R	O	C	K	Y
B	R	A	K	E
E	N	E	M	Y

Q W E R T Y U I O P
A S D F G H J K L
Z X C V B N M

Clue: folders

Puzzle 147

MEDIUM

D	I	M	L	Y	
T	O	D	A	Y	Q W E R T Y U I O P A S D F G H J K L Z X C V B N M
P	U	L	P	Y	
					Clue: gush
S	L	I	C	K	
T	W	E	A	K	Q W E R T Y U I O P A S D F G H J K L Z X C V B N M
L	E	F	T	Y	
					Clue: received
A	G	A	I	N	
P	A	T	I	O	Q W E R T Y U I O P A S D F G H J K L Z X C V B N M
V	O	T	E	R	
					Clue: regulations
C	O	N	C	H	
P	R	A	W	N	Q W E R T Y U I O P A S D F G H J K L Z X C V B N M
E	A	T	E	N	
					Clue: constructed

Puzzle 148

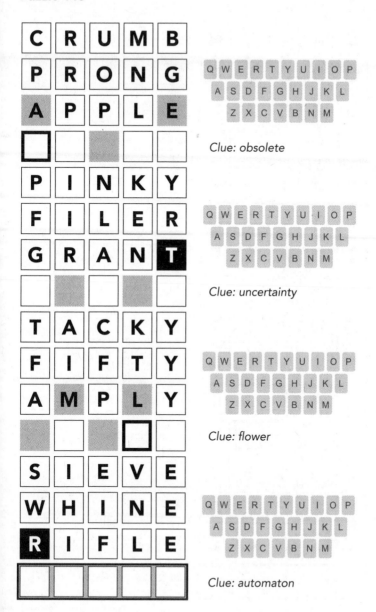

C	R	U	M	B
P	R	O	N	G
A	P	P	L	E

Q W E R T Y U I O P
A S D F G H J K L
Z X C V B N M

Clue: obsolete

P	I	N	K	Y
F	I	L	E	R
G	R	A	N	T

Q W E R T Y U I O P
A S D F G H J K L
Z X C V B N M

Clue: uncertainty

T	A	C	K	Y
F	I	F	T	Y
A	M	P	L	Y

Q W E R T Y U I O P
A S D F G H J K L
Z X C V B N M

Clue: flower

S	I	E	V	E
W	H	I	N	E
R	I	F	L	E

Q W E R T Y U I O P
A S D F G H J K L
Z X C V B N M

Clue: automaton

Puzzle 149

MEDIUM

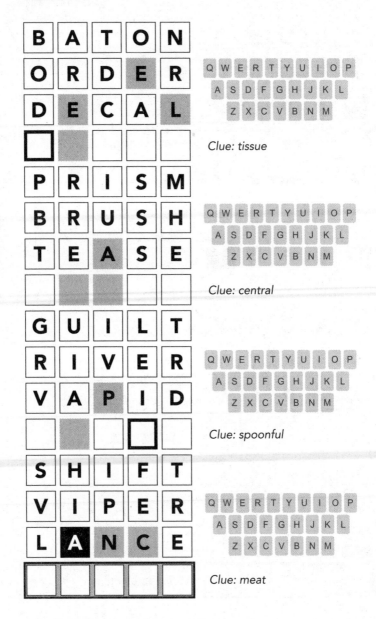

B	A	T	O	N
O	R	D	E	R
D	E	C	A	L

Q W E R T Y U I O P
A S D F G H J K L
Z X C V B N M

Clue: tissue

P	R	I	S	M
B	R	U	S	H
T	E	A	S	E

Q W E R T Y U I O P
A S D F G H J K L
Z X C V B N M

Clue: central

G	U	I	L	T
R	I	V	E	R
V	A	P	I	D

Q W E R T Y U I O P
A S D F G H J K L
Z X C V B N M

Clue: spoonful

S	H	I	F	T
V	I	P	E	R
L	A	N	C	E

Q W E R T Y U I O P
A S D F G H J K L
Z X C V B N M

Clue: meat

Puzzle 150

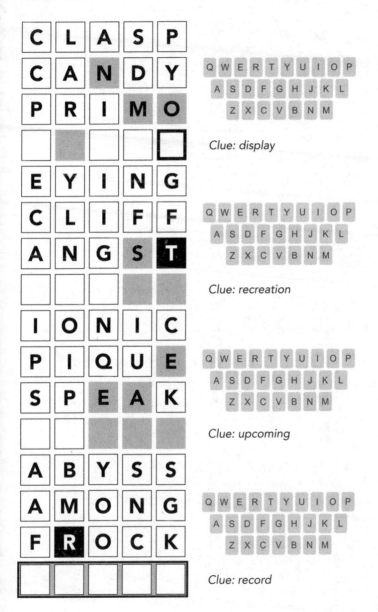

C	L	A	S	P
C	A	N	D	Y
P	R	I	M	O

Q W E R T Y U I O P
A S D F G H J K L
Z X C V B N M

Clue: display

E	Y	I	N	G
C	L	I	F	F
A	N	G	S	T

Q W E R T Y U I O P
A S D F G H J K L
Z X C V B N M

Clue: recreation

I	O	N	I	C
P	I	Q	U	E
S	P	E	A	K

Q W E R T Y U I O P
A S D F G H J K L
Z X C V B N M

Clue: upcoming

A	B	Y	S	S
A	M	O	N	G
F	R	O	C	K

Q W E R T Y U I O P
A S D F G H J K L
Z X C V B N M

Clue: record

MEDIUM

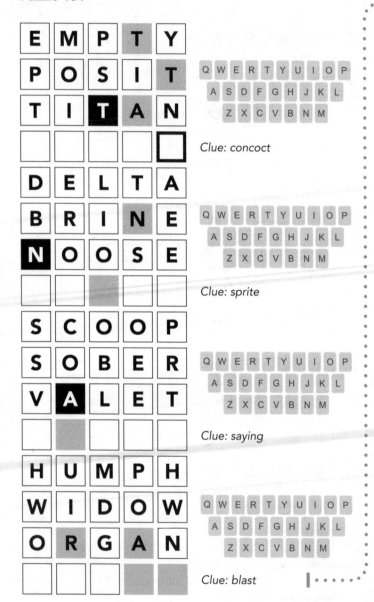

Puzzle 151

E	M	P	T	Y
P	O	S	I	T
T	I	T	A	N
D	E	L	T	A
B	R	I	N	E
N	O	O	S	E
S	C	O	O	P
S	O	B	E	R
V	A	L	E	T
H	U	M	P	H
W	I	D	O	W
O	R	G	A	N

Q W E R T Y U I O P
A S D F G H J K L
Z X C V B N M

Clue: concoct

Q W E R T Y U I O P
A S D F G H J K L
Z X C V B N M

Clue: sprite

Q W E R T Y U I O P
A S D F G H J K L
Z X C V B N M

Clue: saying

Q W E R T Y U I O P
A S D F G H J K L
Z X C V B N M

Clue: blast

EXPERT

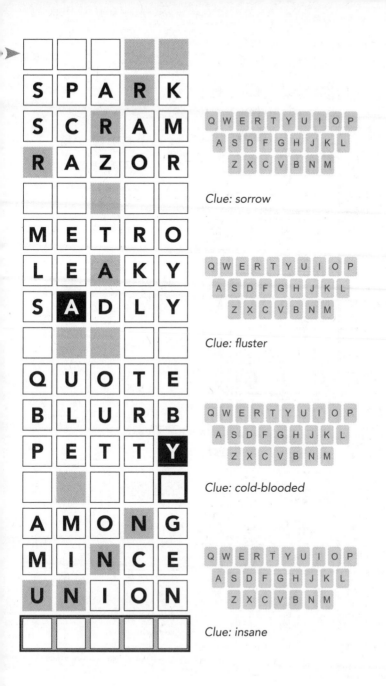

S	P	A	R	K
S	C	R	A	M
R	A	Z	O	R

Q W E R T Y U I O P
A S D F G H J K L
Z X C V B N M

Clue: sorrow

M	E	T	R	O
L	E	A	K	Y
S	A	D	L	Y

Q W E R T Y U I O P
A S D F G H J K L
Z X C V B N M

Clue: fluster

Q	U	O	T	E
B	L	U	R	B
P	E	T	T	Y

Q W E R T Y U I O P
A S D F G H J K L
Z X C V B N M

Clue: cold-blooded

A	M	O	N	G
M	I	N	C	E
U	N	I	O	N

Q W E R T Y U I O P
A S D F G H J K L
Z X C V B N M

Clue: insane

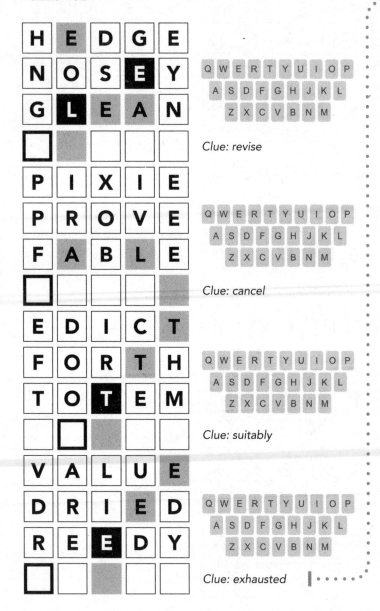

Puzzle 152

H	E	D	G	E
N	O	S	E	Y
G	L	E	A	N

Q W E R T Y U I O P
A S D F G H J K L
Z X C V B N M

Clue: revise

P	I	X	I	E
P	R	O	V	E
F	A	B	L	E

Q W E R T Y U I O P
A S D F G H J K L
Z X C V B N M

Clue: cancel

E	D	I	C	T
F	O	R	T	H
T	O	T	E	M

Q W E R T Y U I O P
A S D F G H J K L
Z X C V B N M

Clue: suitably

V	A	L	U	E
D	R	I	E	D
R	E	E	D	Y

Q W E R T Y U I O P
A S D F G H J K L
Z X C V B N M

Clue: exhausted

EXPERT

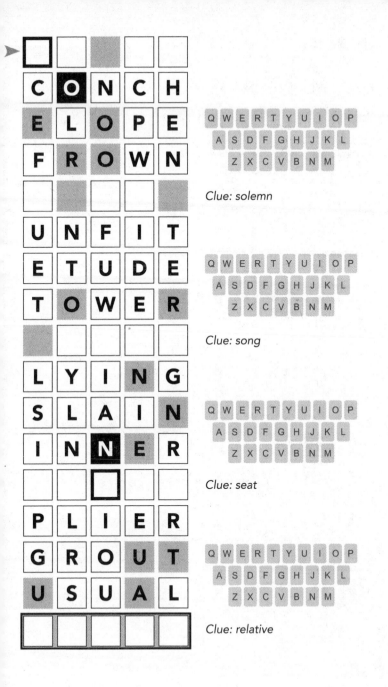

C	O	N	C	H
E	L	O	P	E
F	R	O	W	N

Q W E R T Y U I O P
A S D F G H J K L
Z X C V B N M

Clue: solemn

U	N	F	I	T
E	T	U	D	E
T	O	W	E	R

Q W E R T Y U I O P
A S D F G H J K L
Z X C V B N M

Clue: song

L	Y	I	N	G
S	L	A	I	N
I	N	N	E	R

Q W E R T Y U I O P
A S D F G H J K L
Z X C V B N M

Clue: seat

P	L	I	E	R
G	R	O	U	T
U	S	U	A	L

Q W E R T Y U I O P
A S D F G H J K L
Z X C V B N M

Clue: relative

Puzzle 153

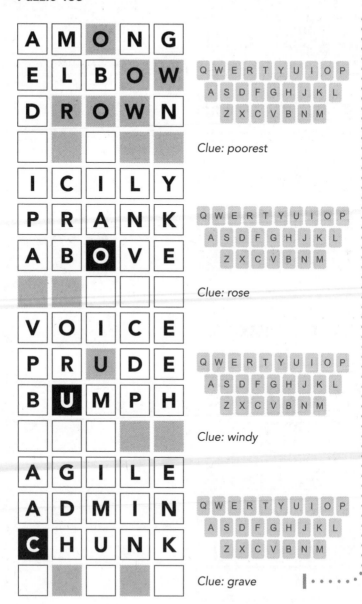

A	M	O	N	G
E	L	B	O	W
D	R	O	W	N

QWERTYUIOP
ASDFGHJKL
ZXCVBNM

Clue: poorest

I	C	I	L	Y
P	R	A	N	K
A	B	O	V	E

QWERTYUIOP
ASDFGHJKL
ZXCVBNM

Clue: rose

V	O	I	C	E
P	R	U	D	E
B	U	M	P	H

QWERTYUIOP
ASDFGHJKL
ZXCVBNM

Clue: windy

A	G	I	L	E
A	D	M	I	N
C	H	U	N	K

QWERTYUIOP
ASDFGHJKL
ZXCVBNM

Clue: grave

EXPERT

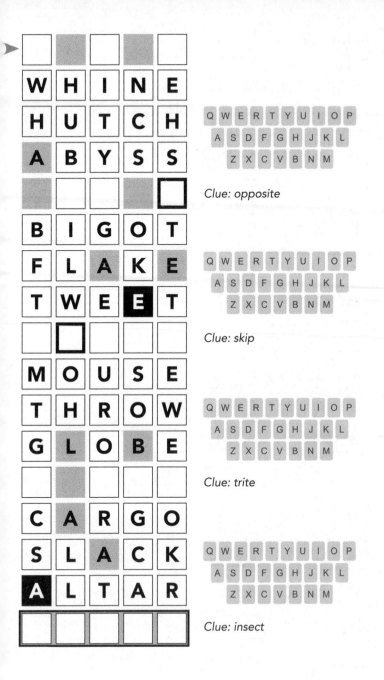

W	H	I	N	E
H	U	T	C	H
A	B	Y	S	S
B	I	G	O	T
F	L	A	K	E
T	W	E	E	T
M	O	U	S	E
T	H	R	O	W
G	L	O	B	E
C	A	R	G	O
S	L	A	C	K
A	L	T	A	R

Q W E R T Y U I O P
A S D F G H J K L
Z X C V B N M

Clue: opposite

Q W E R T Y U I O P
A S D F G H J K L
Z X C V B N M

Clue: skip

Q W E R T Y U I O P
A S D F G H J K L
Z X C V B N M

Clue: trite

Q W E R T Y U I O P
A S D F G H J K L
Z X C V B N M

Clue: insect

EXPERT

EXPERT

Puzzle 154

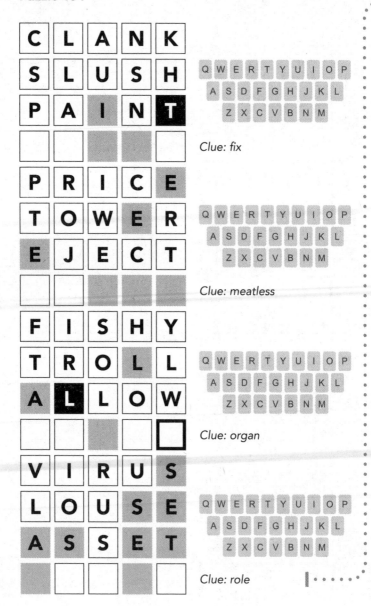

C	L	A	N	K	
S	L	U	S	H	
P	A	I	N	T	
					Clue: *fix*
P	R	I	C	E	
T	O	W	E	R	
E	J	E	C	T	
					Clue: *meatless*
F	I	S	H	Y	
T	R	O	L	L	
A	L	L	O	W	
					Clue: *organ*
V	I	R	U	S	
L	O	U	S	E	
A	S	S	E	T	
					Clue: *role*

Q W E R T Y U I O P
A S D F G H J K L
Z X C V B N M

Q W E R T Y U I O P
A S D F G H J K L
Z X C V B N M

Q W E R T Y U I O P
A S D F G H J K L
Z X C V B N M

Q W E R T Y U I O P
A S D F G H J K L
Z X C V B N M

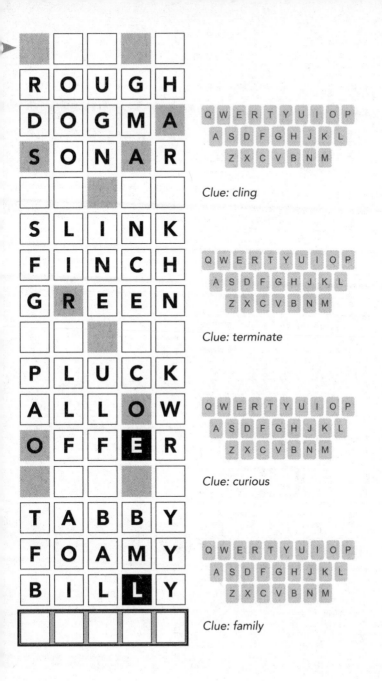

R	O	U	G	H
D	O	G	M	A
S	O	N	A	R

Q W E R T Y U I O P
A S D F G H J K L
Z X C V B N M

Clue: cling

S	L	I	N	K
F	I	N	C	H
G	R	E	E	N

Q W E R T Y U I O P
A S D F G H J K L
Z X C V B N M

Clue: terminate

P	L	U	C	K
A	L	L	O	W
O	F	F	E	R

Q W E R T Y U I O P
A S D F G H J K L
Z X C V B N M

Clue: curious

T	A	B	B	Y
F	O	A	M	Y
B	I	L	L	Y

Q W E R T Y U I O P
A S D F G H J K L
Z X C V B N M

Clue: family

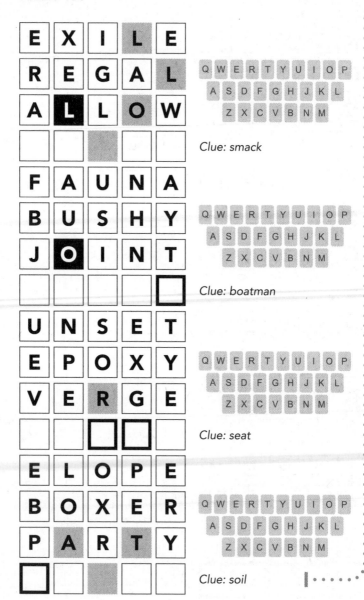

Puzzle 155

E	X	I	L	E
R	E	G	A	L
A	L	L	O	W

QWERTYUIOP
ASDFGHJKL
ZXCVBNM

Clue: smack

F	A	U	N	A
B	U	S	H	Y
J	O	I	N	T

QWERTYUIOP
ASDFGHJKL
ZXCVBNM

Clue: boatman

U	N	S	E	T
E	P	O	X	Y
V	E	R	G	E

QWERTYUIOP
ASDFGHJKL
ZXCVBNM

Clue: seat

E	L	O	P	E
B	O	X	E	R
P	A	R	T	Y

QWERTYUIOP
ASDFGHJKL
ZXCVBNM

Clue: soil

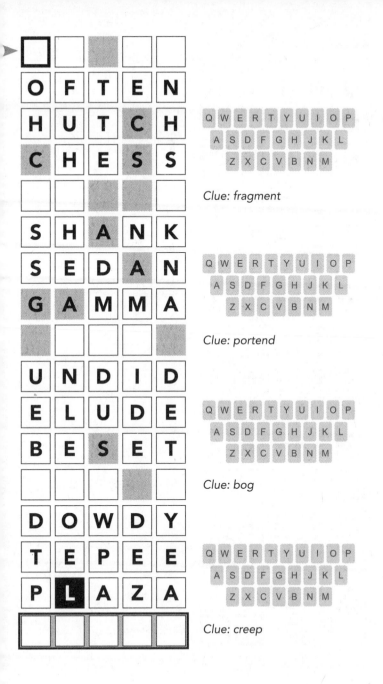

O	F	T	E	N
H	U	T	C	H
C	H	E	S	S
S	H	A	N	K
S	E	D	A	N
G	A	M	M	A
U	N	D	I	D
E	L	U	D	E
B	E	S	E	T
D	O	W	D	Y
T	E	P	E	E
P	L	A	Z	A

Q W E R T Y U I O P
A S D F G H J K L
Z X C V B N M

Clue: fragment

Q W E R T Y U I O P
A S D F G H J K L
Z X C V B N M

Clue: portend

Q W E R T Y U I O P
A S D F G H J K L
Z X C V B N M

Clue: bog

Q W E R T Y U I O P
A S D F G H J K L
Z X C V B N M

Clue: creep

EXPERT

Puzzle 156

U	N	I	O	N
M	E	R	I	T
N	E	W	L	Y

Q W E R T Y U I O P
A S D F G H J K L
Z X C V B N M

Clue: peeling

V	O	C	A	L
T	R	A	I	N
A	L	P	H	A

Q W E R T Y U I O P
A S D F G H J K L
Z X C V B N M

Clue: creditor

P	E	N	N	E
P	H	A	S	E
C	I	D	E	R

Q W E R T Y U I O P
A S D F G H J K L
Z X C V B N M

Clue: modestly

B	R	O	A	D
R	U	M	B	A
A	V	A	I	L

Q W E R T Y U I O P
A S D F G H J K L
Z X C V B N M

Clue: incantation

EXPERT

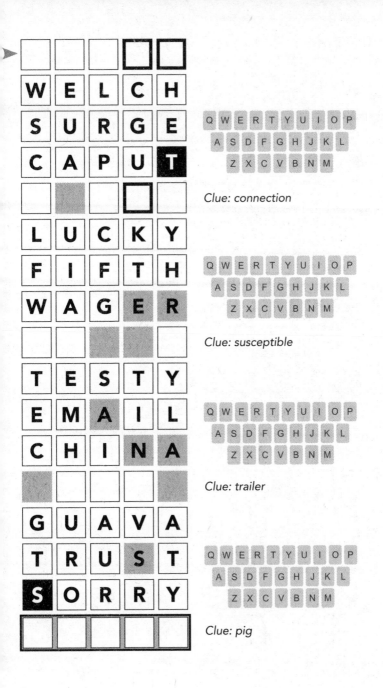

W	E	L	C	H
S	U	R	G	E
C	A	P	U	T
L	U	C	K	Y
F	I	F	T	H
W	A	G	E	R
T	E	S	T	Y
E	M	A	I	L
C	H	I	N	A
G	U	A	V	A
T	R	U	S	T
S	O	R	R	Y

Q W E R T Y U I O P
A S D F G H J K L
Z X C V B N M

Clue: connection

Q W E R T Y U I O P
A S D F G H J K L
Z X C V B N M

Clue: susceptible

Q W E R T Y U I O P
A S D F G H J K L
Z X C V B N M

Clue: trailer

Q W E R T Y U I O P
A S D F G H J K L
Z X C V B N M

Clue: pig

EXPERT

EXPERT

Puzzle 157

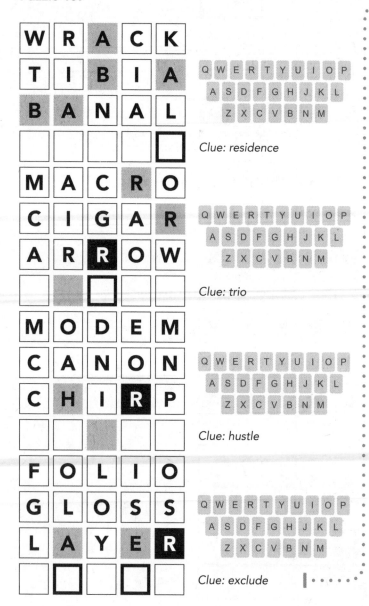

W	R	A	C	K
T	I	B	I	A
B	A	N	A	L

Q W E R T Y U I O P
A S D F G H J K L
Z X C V B N M

Clue: residence

M	A	C	R	O
C	I	G	A	R
A	R	R	O	W

Q W E R T Y U I O P
A S D F G H J K L
Z X C V B N M

Clue: trio

M	O	D	E	M
C	A	N	O	N
C	H	I	R	P

Q W E R T Y U I O P
A S D F G H J K L
Z X C V B N M

Clue: hustle

F	O	L	I	O
G	L	O	S	S
L	A	Y	E	R

Q W E R T Y U I O P
A S D F G H J K L
Z X C V B N M

Clue: exclude

S	H	R	U	B
C	R	I	M	P
L	U	M	P	Y
P	A	P	A	L
C	H	E	E	K
D	U	N	C	E
C	L	A	S	H
T	A	W	N	Y
N	I	N	J	A
I	N	L	A	Y
C	A	U	L	K
D	R	A	M	A

Q W E R T Y U I O P
A S D F G H J K L
Z X C V B N M

Clue: disciplinary

Q W E R T Y U I O P
A S D F G H J K L
Z X C V B N M

Clue: sarcasm

Q W E R T Y U I O P
A S D F G H J K L
Z X C V B N M

Clue: proprietor

Q W E R T Y U I O P
A S D F G H J K L
Z X C V B N M

Clue: resulted

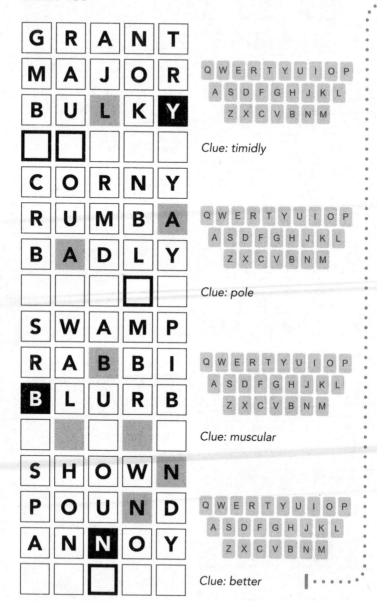

Puzzle 158

G	R	A	N	T
M	A	J	O	R
B	U	L	K	Y
C	O	R	N	Y
R	U	M	B	A
B	A	D	L	Y
S	W	A	M	P
R	A	B	B	I
B	L	U	R	B
S	H	O	W	N
P	O	U	N	D
A	N	N	O	Y

Q W E R T Y U I O P
A S D F G H J K L
Z X C V B N M

Clue: timidly

Q W E R T Y U I O P
A S D F G H J K L
Z X C V B N M

Clue: pole

Q W E R T Y U I O P
A S D F G H J K L
Z X C V B N M

Clue: muscular

Q W E R T Y U I O P
A S D F G H J K L
Z X C V B N M

Clue: better

EXPERT

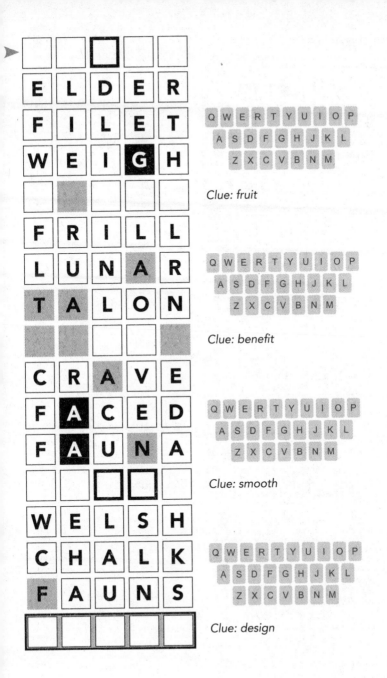

E	L	D	E	R
F	I	L	E	T
W	E	I	G	H

Q W E R T Y U I O P
A S D F G H J K L
Z X C V B N M

Clue: fruit

F	R	I	L	L
L	U	N	A	R
T	A	L	O	N

Q W E R T Y U I O P
A S D F G H J K L
Z X C V B N M

Clue: benefit

C	R	A	V	E
F	A	C	E	D
F	A	U	N	A

Q W E R T Y U I O P
A S D F G H J K L
Z X C V B N M

Clue: smooth

W	E	L	S	H
C	H	A	L	K
F	A	U	N	S

Q W E R T Y U I O P
A S D F G H J K L
Z X C V B N M

Clue: design

EXPERT

Puzzle 159

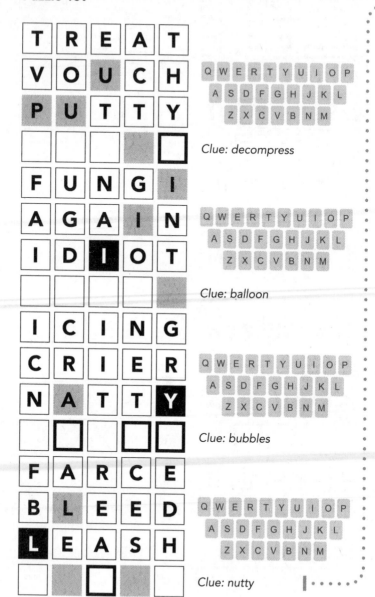

T	R	E	A	T	
V	O	U	C	H	
P	U	T	T	Y	
					Clue: decompress
F	U	N	G	I	
A	G	A	I	N	
I	D	I	O	T	
					Clue: balloon
I	C	I	N	G	
C	R	I	E	R	
N	A	T	T	Y	
					Clue: bubbles
F	A	R	C	E	
B	L	E	E	D	
L	E	A	S	H	
					Clue: nutty

Q W E R T Y U I O P
A S D F G H J K L
Z X C V B N M

Q W E R T Y U I O P
A S D F G H J K L
Z X C V B N M

Q W E R T Y U I O P
A S D F G H J K L
Z X C V B N M

Q W E R T Y U I O P
A S D F G H J K L
Z X C V B N M

EXPERT

R	E	H	A	B
A	V	A	I	L
S	W	E	E	T

Q W E R T Y U I O P
A S D F G H J K L
Z X C V B N M

Clue: utensil

F	E	I	G	N
C	O	U	C	H
B	A	L	M	Y

Q W E R T Y U I O P
A S D F G H J K L
Z X C V B N M

Clue: modify

L	I	G	H	T
S	L	O	O	P
P	L	U	N	K

Q W E R T Y U I O P
A S D F G H J K L
Z X C V B N M

Clue: mash

V	A	L	U	E
A	B	B	E	Y
N	E	E	D	Y

Q W E R T Y U I O P
A S D F G H J K L
Z X C V B N M

Clue: decimal

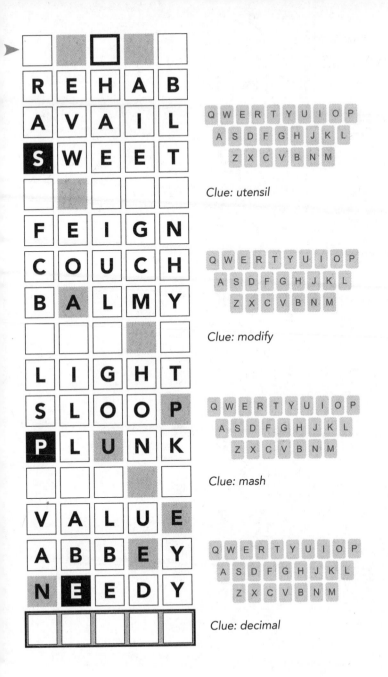

Puzzle 160

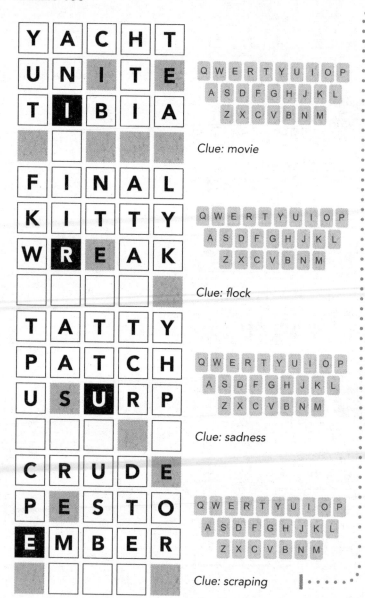

Y	A	C	H	T
U	N	I	T	E
T	I	B	I	A

Q W E R T Y U I O P
A S D F G H J K L
Z X C V B N M

Clue: movie

F	I	N	A	L
K	I	T	T	Y
W	R	E	A	K

Q W E R T Y U I O P
A S D F G H J K L
Z X C V B N M

Clue: flock

T	A	T	T	Y
P	A	T	C	H
U	S	U	R	P

Q W E R T Y U I O P
A S D F G H J K L
Z X C V B N M

Clue: sadness

C	R	U	D	E
P	E	S	T	O
E	M	B	E	R

Q W E R T Y U I O P
A S D F G H J K L
Z X C V B N M

Clue: scraping

EXPERT

T	R	U	T	H
T	I	P	S	Y
S	H	E	L	F
U	N	D	I	D
R	O	G	U	E
S	I	E	G	E
D	R	U	I	D
E	X	U	L	T
W	A	C	K	Y
S	H	O	R	N
M	A	D	A	M
C	U	R	V	E

Q W E R T Y U I O P
A S D F G H J K L
Z X C V B N M

Clue: pin

Q W E R T Y U I O P
A S D F G H J K L
Z X C V B N M

Clue: troublesome

Q W E R T Y U I O P
A S D F G H J K L
Z X C V B N M

Clue: frighten

Q W E R T Y U I O P
A S D F G H J K L
Z X C V B N M

Clue: provoke

EXPERT

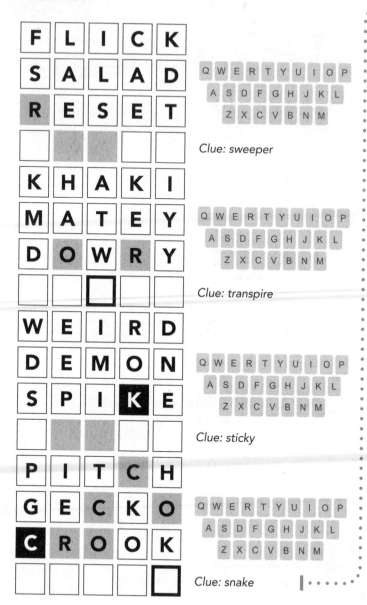

Puzzle 161

F	L	I	C	K
S	A	L	A	D
R	E	S	E	T

Q W E R T Y U I O P
A S D F G H J K L
Z X C V B N M

Clue: sweeper

K	H	A	K	I
M	A	T	E	Y
D	O	W	R	Y

Q W E R T Y U I O P
A S D F G H J K L
Z X C V B N M

Clue: transpire

W	E	I	R	D
D	E	M	O	N
S	P	I	K	E

Q W E R T Y U I O P
A S D F G H J K L
Z X C V B N M

Clue: sticky

P	I	T	C	H
G	E	C	K	O
C	R	O	O	K

Q W E R T Y U I O P
A S D F G H J K L
Z X C V B N M

Clue: snake

EXPERT

T	H	E	I	R
S	U	S	H	I
I	D	I	O	M
F	E	R	R	Y
C	R	I	E	D
T	H	I	N	K
A	M	A	Z	E
R	E	C	U	R
U	S	H	E	R
G	R	E	E	N
S	E	I	Z	E
P	E	D	A	L

Q W E R T Y U I O P
A S D F G H J K L
Z X C V B N M

Clue: house

Q W E R T Y U I O P
A S D F G H J K L
Z X C V B N M

Clue: spirit

Q W E R T Y U I O P
A S D F G H J K L
Z X C V B N M

Clue: fail

Q W E R T Y U I O P
A S D F G H J K L
Z X C V B N M

Clue: dots

EXPERT

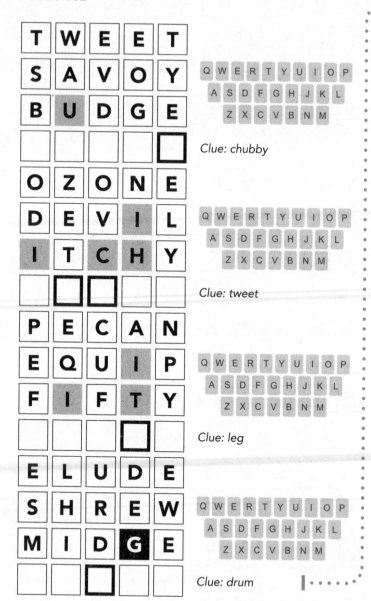

Puzzle 162

T	W	E	E	T
S	A	V	O	Y
B	U	D	G	E
O	Z	O	N	E
D	E	V	I	L
I	T	C	H	Y
P	E	C	A	N
E	Q	U	I	P
F	I	F	T	Y
E	L	U	D	E
S	H	R	E	W
M	I	D	G	E

Q W E R T Y U I O P
A S D F G H J K L
Z X C V B N M

Clue: chubby

Q W E R T Y U I O P
A S D F G H J K L
Z X C V B N M

Clue: tweet

Q W E R T Y U I O P
A S D F G H J K L
Z X C V B N M

Clue: leg

Q W E R T Y U I O P
A S D F G H J K L
Z X C V B N M

Clue: drum

EXPERT

G	A	M	M	A
B	R	A	S	S
S	P	I	E	D
S	T	A	F	F
S	H	E	E	T
B	E	L	L	S
R	E	A	R	M
M	I	N	T	Y
B	L	O	C	K
I	V	O	R	Y
R	E	T	R	Y
S	H	I	N	Y

Q W E R T Y U I O P
A S D F G H J K L
Z X C V B N M

Clue: barrier

Q W E R T Y U I O P
A S D F G H J K L
Z X C V B N M

Clue: repeat

Q W E R T Y U I O P
A S D F G H J K L
Z X C V B N M

Clue: frown

Q W E R T Y U I O P
A S D F G H J K L
Z X C V B N M

Clue: foreign

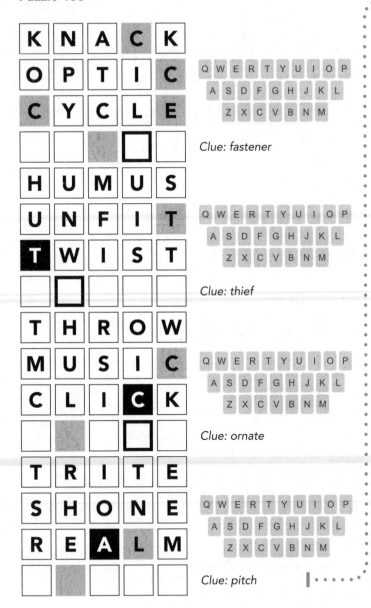

EXPERT

Puzzle 163

K	N	A	C	K
O	P	T	I	C
C	Y	C	L	E

Q W E R T Y U I O P
A S D F G H J K L
Z X C V B N M

Clue: fastener

H	U	M	U	S
U	N	F	I	T
T	W	I	S	T

Q W E R T Y U I O P
A S D F G H J K L
Z X C V B N M

Clue: thief

T	H	R	O	W
M	U	S	I	C
C	L	I	C	K

Q W E R T Y U I O P
A S D F G H J K L
Z X C V B N M

Clue: ornate

T	R	I	T	E
S	H	O	N	E
R	E	A	L	M

Q W E R T Y U I O P
A S D F G H J K L
Z X C V B N M

Clue: pitch

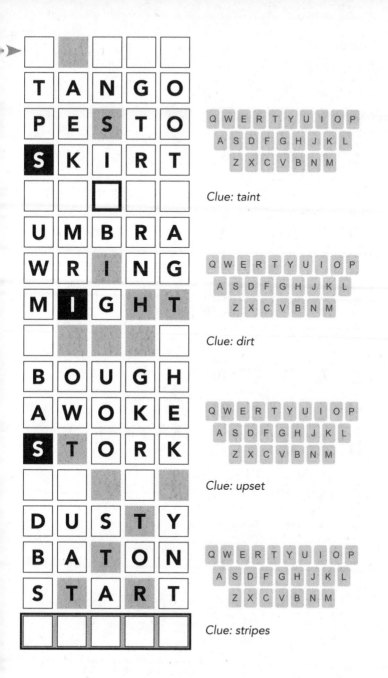

T	A	N	G	O
P	E	S	T	O
S	K	I	R	T

Q W E R T Y U I O P
A S D F G H J K L
Z X C V B N M

Clue: taint

U	M	B	R	A
W	R	I	N	G
M	I	G	H	T

Q W E R T Y U I O P
A S D F G H J K L
Z X C V B N M

Clue: dirt

B	O	U	G	H
A	W	O	K	E
S	T	O	R	K

Q W E R T Y U I O P
A S D F G H J K L
Z X C V B N M

Clue: upset

D	U	S	T	Y
B	A	T	O	N
S	T	A	R	T

Q W E R T Y U I O P
A S D F G H J K L
Z X C V B N M

Clue: stripes

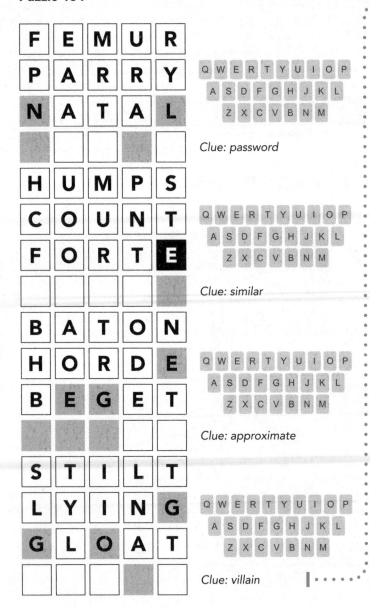

EXPERT

Puzzle 164

F	E	M	U	R
P	A	R	R	Y
N	A	T	A	L

Q W E R T Y U I O P
A S D F G H J K L
Z X C V B N M

Clue: password

H	U	M	P	S
C	O	U	N	T
F	O	R	T	E

Q W E R T Y U I O P
A S D F G H J K L
Z X C V B N M

Clue: similar

B	A	T	O	N
H	O	R	D	E
B	E	G	E	T

Q W E R T Y U I O P
A S D F G H J K L
Z X C V B N M

Clue: approximate

S	T	I	L	T
L	Y	I	N	G
G	L	O	A	T

Q W E R T Y U I O P
A S D F G H J K L
Z X C V B N M

Clue: villain

F	R	E	E	D
S	N	E	A	K
U	S	U	R	P

Q W E R T Y U I O P
A S D F G H J K L
Z X C V B N M

Clue: masculine

T	H	I	N	G
S	I	R	E	N
E	N	N	U	I

Q W E R T Y U I O P
A S D F G H J K L
Z X C V B N M

Clue: instrument

G	R	E	E	T
M	U	R	A	L
S	C	A	R	Y

Q W E R T Y U I O P
A S D F G H J K L
Z X C V B N M

Clue: wireless

F	O	C	U	S
P	U	L	P	Y
G	R	O	A	N

Q W E R T Y U I O P
A S D F G H J K L
Z X C V B N M

Clue: conscious

Puzzle 165

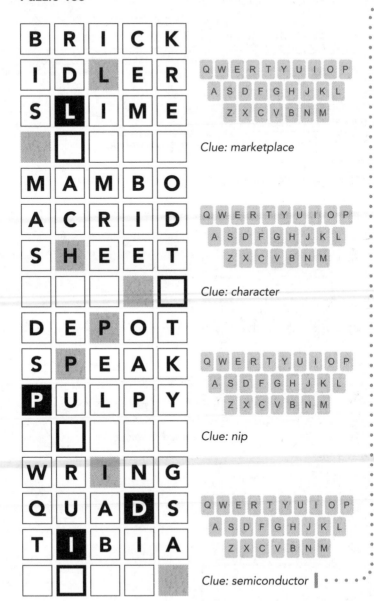

B	R	I	C	K	
I	D	L	E	R	
S	L	I	M	E	
					Clue: marketplace
M	A	M	B	O	
A	C	R	I	D	
S	H	E	E	T	
					Clue: character
D	E	P	O	T	
S	P	E	A	K	
P	U	L	P	Y	
					Clue: nip
W	R	I	N	G	
Q	U	A	D	S	
T	I	B	I	A	
					Clue: semiconductor

Q W E R T Y U I O P
A S D F G H J K L
Z X C V B N M

Q W E R T Y U I O P
A S D F G H J K L
Z X C V B N M

Q W E R T Y U I O P
A S D F G H J K L
Z X C V B N M

Q W E R T Y U I O P
A S D F G H J K L
Z X C V B N M

EXPERT

S	N	O	W	Y
T	O	N	A	L
P	L	A	C	E
M	A	F	I	A
A	O	R	T	A
T	R	E	N	D
B	E	A	S	T
C	L	A	S	H
E	V	E	R	Y
B	A	N	A	L
S	T	O	O	D
F	O	L	I	O

Q W E R T Y U I O P
A S D F G H J K L
Z X C V B N M

Clue: grinder

Q W E R T Y U I O P
A S D F G H J K L
Z X C V B N M

Clue: unrefined

Q W E R T Y U I O P
A S D F G H J K L
Z X C V B N M

Clue: dog

Q W E R T Y U I O P
A S D F G H J K L
Z X C V B N M

Clue: change

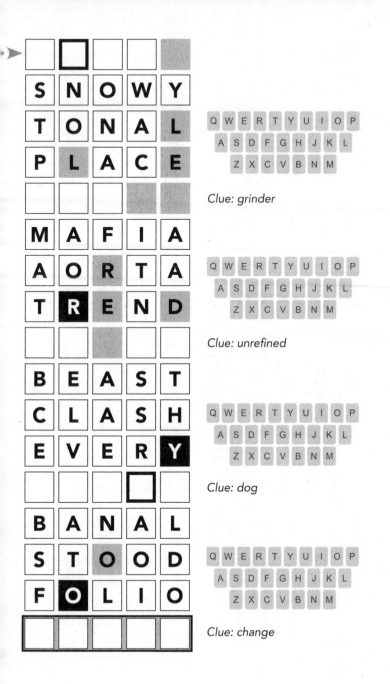

Puzzle 166

T	R	A	C	K	
N	O	B	L	E	Q W E R T Y U I O P A S D F G H J K L Z X C V B N M
O	L	I	V	E	
					Clue: prickly
T	U	N	I	C	
V	O	I	C	E	Q W E R T Y U I O P A S D F G H J K L Z X C V B N M
E	M	C	E	E	
					Clue: electronic
C	O	U	C	H	
T	A	T	T	Y	Q W E R T Y U I O P A S D F G H J K L Z X C V B N M
C	R	I	M	E	
					Clue: temperature
F	A	T	T	Y	
C	H	O	R	D	Q W E R T Y U I O P A S D F G H J K L Z X C V B N M
D	R	O	S	S	
					Clue: danger

EXPERT

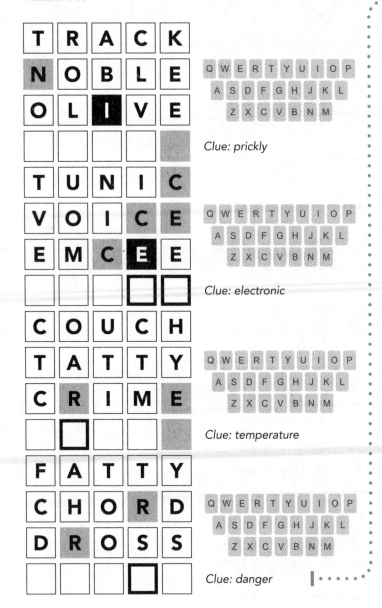

L	E	G	A	L	
F	L	A	R	E	Q W E R T Y U I O P
A	R	O	M	A	A S D F G H J K L Z X C V B N M
					Clue: custom
B	U	N	N	Y	
L	A	D	E	N	Q W E R T Y U I O P A S D F G H J K L
S	T	A	T	E	Z X C V B N M
					Clue: underground
S	E	D	A	N	
P	A	P	A	L	Q W E R T Y U I O P
B	E	A	C	H	A S D F G H J K L Z X C V B N M
					Clue: foam
N	A	T	A	L	
F	L	I	N	G	Q W E R T Y U I O P A S D F G H J K L
H	O	U	N	D	Z X C V B N M
					Clue: customer

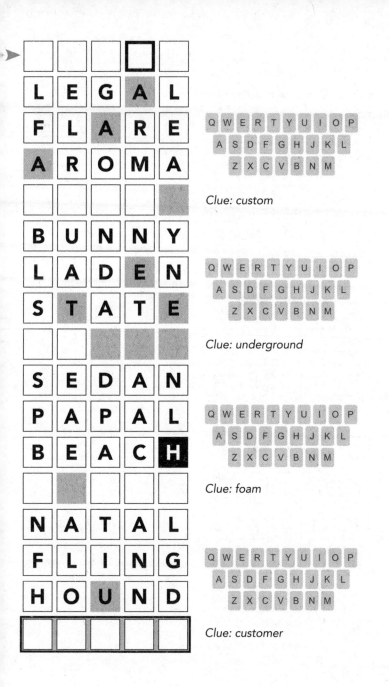

EXPERT

EXPERT

Puzzle 167

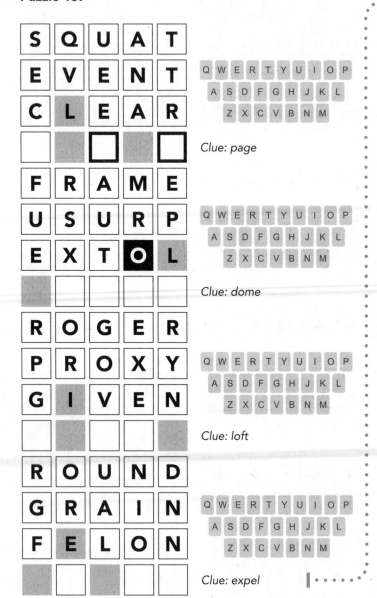

S	Q	U	A	T	
E	V	E	N	T	QWERTYUIOP
C	L	E	A	R	ASDFGHJKL ZXCVBNM
					Clue: page
F	R	A	M	E	
U	S	U	R	P	QWERTYUIOP
E	X	T	O	L	ASDFGHJKL ZXCVBNM
					Clue: dome
R	O	G	E	R	
P	R	O	X	Y	QWERTYUIOP
G	I	V	E	N	ASDFGHJKL ZXCVBNM
					Clue: loft
R	O	U	N	D	
G	R	A	I	N	QWERTYUIOP
F	E	L	O	N	ASDFGHJKL ZXCVBNM
					Clue: expel

C	A	D	D	Y
W	O	M	A	N
O	X	I	D	E

Q W E R T Y U I O P
A S D F G H J K L
Z X C V B N M

Clue: contradict

B	I	N	G	E
R	U	R	A	L
B	A	L	M	Y

Q W E R T Y U I O P
A S D F G H J K L
Z X C V B N M

Clue: enough

S	H	I	N	Y
K	N	O	W	N
C	L	I	C	K

Q W E R T Y U I O P
A S D F G H J K L
Z X C V B N M

Clue: sadder

K	N	A	V	E
C	A	R	V	E
A	H	E	A	D

Q W E R T Y U I O P
A S D F G H J K L
Z X C V B N M

Clue: defence

EXPERT

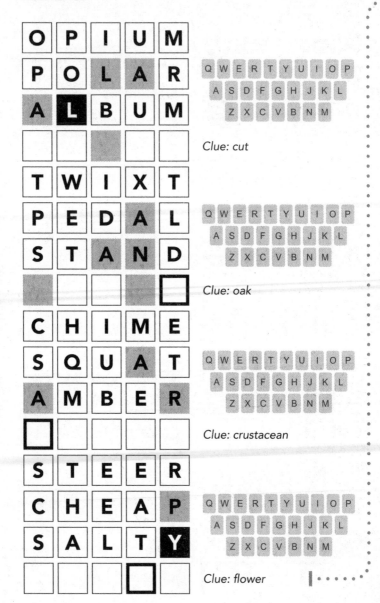

Puzzle 168

O	P	I	U	M
P	O	L	A	R
A	L	B	U	M

Q W E R T Y U I O P
A S D F G H J K L
Z X C V B N M

Clue: cut

T	W	I	X	T
P	E	D	A	L
S	T	A	N	D

Q W E R T Y U I O P
A S D F G H J K L
Z X C V B N M

Clue: oak

C	H	I	M	E
S	Q	U	A	T
A	M	B	E	R

Q W E R T Y U I O P
A S D F G H J K L
Z X C V B N M

Clue: crustacean

S	T	E	E	R
C	H	E	A	P
S	A	L	T	Y

Q W E R T Y U I O P
A S D F G H J K L
Z X C V B N M

Clue: flower

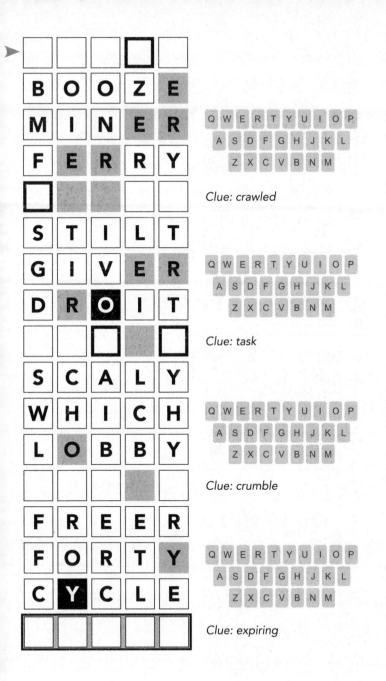

B	O	O	Z	E
M	I	N	E	R
F	E	R	R	Y
S	T	I	L	T
G	I	V	E	R
D	R	O	I	T
S	C	A	L	Y
W	H	I	C	H
L	O	B	B	Y
F	R	E	E	R
F	O	R	T	Y
C	Y	C	L	E

Q W E R T Y U I O P
A S D F G H J K L
Z X C V B N M

Clue: crawled

Q W E R T Y U I O P
A S D F G H J K L
Z X C V B N M

Clue: task

Q W E R T Y U I O P
A S D F G H J K L
Z X C V B N M

Clue: crumble

Q W E R T Y U I O P
A S D F G H J K L
Z X C V B N M

Clue: expiring

EXPERT

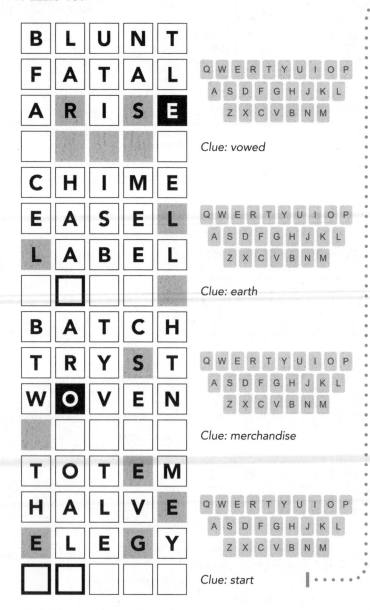

Puzzle 169

B	L	U	N	T
F	A	T	A	L
A	R	I	S	E

QWERTYUIOP
ASDFGHJKL
ZXCVBNM

Clue: vowed

C	H	I	M	E
E	A	S	E	L
L	A	B	E	L

QWERTYUIOP
ASDFGHJKL
ZXCVBNM

Clue: earth

B	A	T	C	H
T	R	Y	S	T
W	O	V	E	N

QWERTYUIOP
ASDFGHJKL
ZXCVBNM

Clue: merchandise

T	O	T	E	M
H	A	L	V	E
E	L	E	G	Y

QWERTYUIOP
ASDFGHJKL
ZXCVBNM

Clue: start

EXPERT

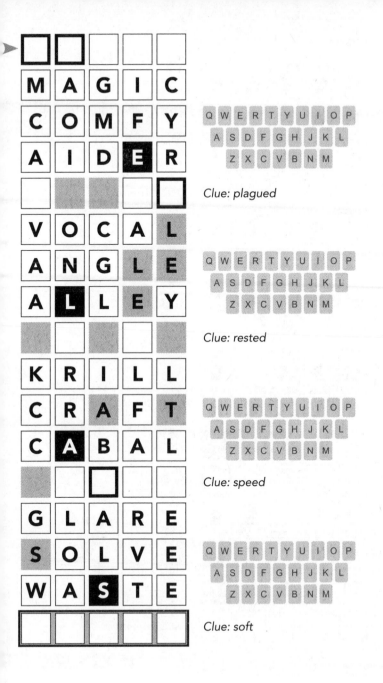

M	A	G	I	C	
C	O	M	F	Y	
A	I	D	E	R	
					Clue: plagued
V	O	C	A	L	
A	N	G	L	E	
A	L	L	E	Y	
					Clue: rested
K	R	I	L	L	
C	R	A	F	T	
C	A	B	A	L	
					Clue: speed
G	L	A	R	E	
S	O	L	V	E	
W	A	S	T	E	
					Clue: soft

Q W E R T Y U I O P
A S D F G H J K L
Z X C V B N M

Clue: plagued

Q W E R T Y U I O P
A S D F G H J K L
Z X C V B N M

Clue: rested

Q W E R T Y U I O P
A S D F G H J K L
Z X C V B N M

Clue: speed

Q W E R T Y U I O P
A S D F G H J K L
Z X C V B N M

Clue: soft

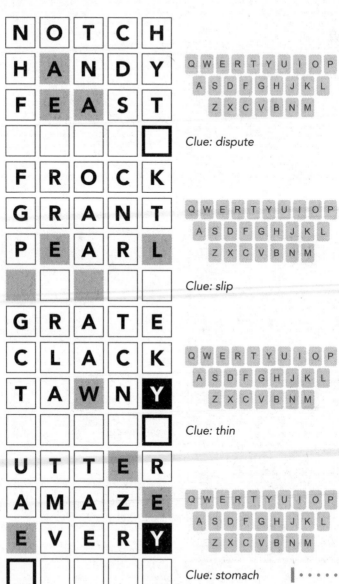

Puzzle 170

N	O	T	C	H
H	A	N	D	Y
F	E	A	S	T

QWERTYUIOP
ASDFGHJKL
ZXCVBNM

Clue: dispute

F	R	O	C	K
G	R	A	N	T
P	E	A	R	L

QWERTYUIOP
ASDFGHJKL
ZXCVBNM

Clue: slip

G	R	A	T	E
C	L	A	C	K
T	A	W	N	Y

QWERTYUIOP
ASDFGHJKL
ZXCVBNM

Clue: thin

U	T	T	E	R
A	M	A	Z	E
E	V	E	R	Y

QWERTYUIOP
ASDFGHJKL
ZXCVBNM

Clue: stomach

EXPERT

S	T	R	I	P
L	U	N	A	R
A	W	A	R	D

Q W E R T Y U I O P
A S D F G H J K L
Z X C V B N M

Clue: mind

B	R	I	C	K
S	T	R	U	T
H	O	N	E	Y

Q W E R T Y U I O P
A S D F G H J K L
Z X C V B N M

Clue: tug

W	H	O	O	P
C	O	R	E	R
R	E	T	R	Y

Q W E R T Y U I O P
A S D F G H J K L
Z X C V B N M

Clue: competitor

A	C	U	T	E
C	H	O	R	E
E	N	E	M	Y

Q W E R T Y U I O P
A S D F G H J K L
Z X C V B N M

Clue: husk

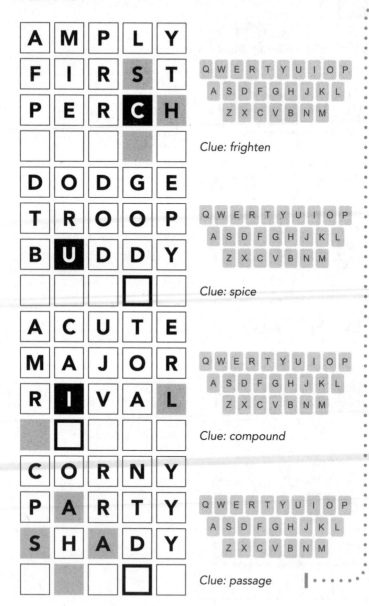

Puzzle 171

A	M	P	L	Y
F	I	R	S	T
P	E	R	C	H

Q W E R T Y U I O P
A S D F G H J K L
Z X C V B N M

Clue: frighten

D	O	D	G	E
T	R	O	O	P
B	U	D	D	Y

Q W E R T Y U I O P
A S D F G H J K L
Z X C V B N M

Clue: spice

A	C	U	T	E
M	A	J	O	R
R	I	V	A	L

Q W E R T Y U I O P
A S D F G H J K L
Z X C V B N M

Clue: compound

C	O	R	N	Y
P	A	R	T	Y
S	H	A	D	Y

Q W E R T Y U I O P
A S D F G H J K L
Z X C V B N M

Clue: passage

EXPERT

Z	E	S	T	Y
R	E	H	A	B
B	L	U	F	F
E	X	A	C	T
W	R	I	T	E
O	T	T	E	R
O	T	H	E	R
S	H	A	R	D
A	R	R	A	Y
P	O	U	N	D
H	O	R	D	E
T	O	T	E	M

Q W E R T Y U I O P
A S D F G H J K L
Z X C V B N M

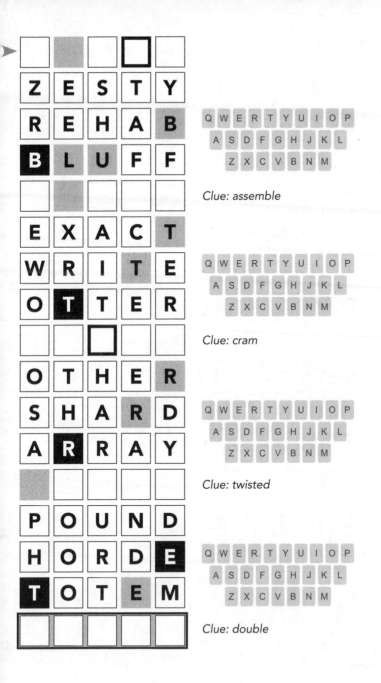

Clue: assemble

Q W E R T Y U I O P
A S D F G H J K L
Z X C V B N M

Clue: cram

Q W E R T Y U I O P
A S D F G H J K L
Z X C V B N M

Clue: twisted

Q W E R T Y U I O P
A S D F G H J K L
Z X C V B N M

Clue: double

Puzzle 172

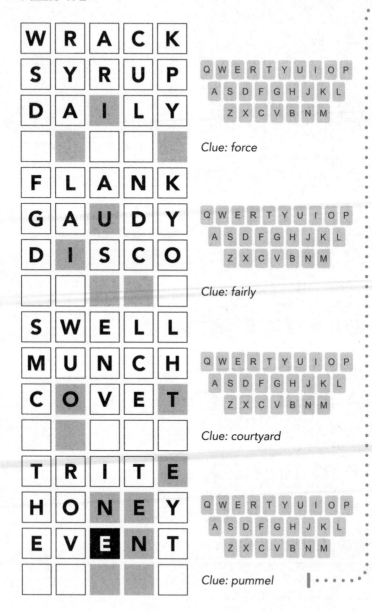

EXPERT

W	R	A	C	K
S	Y	R	U	P
D	A	I	L	Y

Q W E R T Y U I O P
A S D F G H J K L
Z X C V B N M

Clue: force

F	L	A	N	K
G	A	U	D	Y
D	I	S	C	O

Q W E R T Y U I O P
A S D F G H J K L
Z X C V B N M

Clue: fairly

S	W	E	L	L
M	U	N	C	H
C	O	V	E	T

Q W E R T Y U I O P
A S D F G H J K L
Z X C V B N M

Clue: courtyard

T	R	I	T	E
H	O	N	E	Y
E	V	E	N	T

Q W E R T Y U I O P
A S D F G H J K L
Z X C V B N M

Clue: pummel

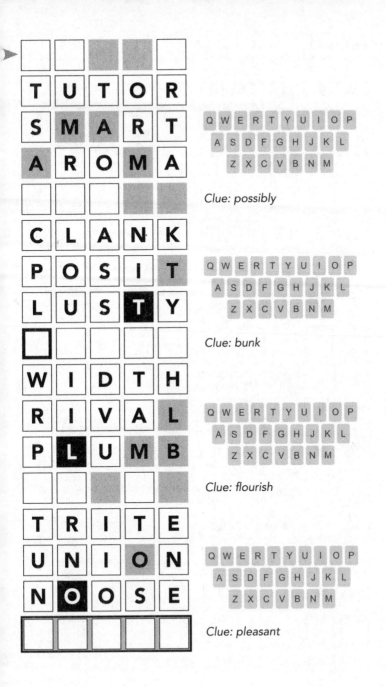

T	U	T	O	R
S	M	A	R	T
A	R	O	M	A
C	L	A	N	K
P	O	S	I	T
L	U	S	T	Y
W	I	D	T	H
R	I	V	A	L
P	L	U	M	B
T	R	I	T	E
U	N	I	O	N
N	O	O	S	E

Q W E R T Y U I O P
A S D F G H J K L
Z X C V B N M

Clue: possibly

Q W E R T Y U I O P
A S D F G H J K L
Z X C V B N M

Clue: bunk

Q W E R T Y U I O P
A S D F G H J K L
Z X C V B N M

Clue: flourish

Q W E R T Y U I O P
A S D F G H J K L
Z X C V B N M

Clue: pleasant

EXPERT

Puzzle 173

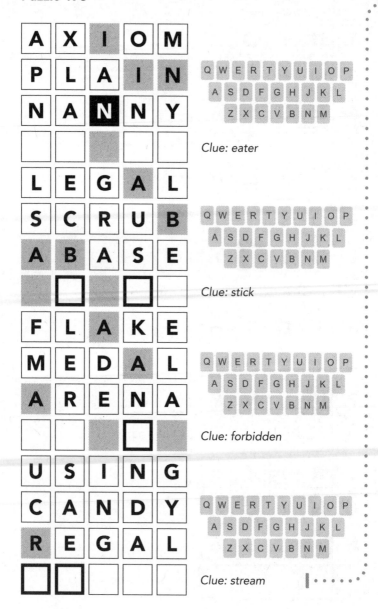

A	X	I	O	M
P	L	A	I	N
N	A	N	N	Y

Q W E R T Y U I O P
A S D F G H J K L
Z X C V B N M

Clue: eater

L	E	G	A	L
S	C	R	U	B
A	B	A	S	E

Q W E R T Y U I O P
A S D F G H J K L
Z X C V B N M

Clue: stick

F	L	A	K	E
M	E	D	A	L
A	R	E	N	A

Q W E R T Y U I O P
A S D F G H J K L
Z X C V B N M

Clue: forbidden

U	S	I	N	G
C	A	N	D	Y
R	E	G	A	L

Q W E R T Y U I O P
A S D F G H J K L
Z X C V B N M

Clue: stream

EXPERT

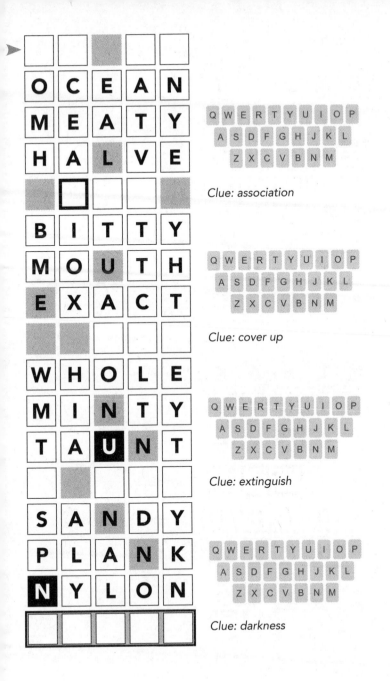

O	C	E	A	N
M	E	A	T	Y
H	A	L	V	E
B	I	T	T	Y
M	O	U	T	H
E	X	A	C	T
W	H	O	L	E
M	I	N	T	Y
T	A	U	N	T
S	A	N	D	Y
P	L	A	N	K
N	Y	L	O	N

Q W E R T Y U I O P
A S D F G H J K L
Z X C V B N M

Clue: association

Q W E R T Y U I O P
A S D F G H J K L
Z X C V B N M

Clue: cover up

Q W E R T Y U I O P
A S D F G H J K L
Z X C V B N M

Clue: extinguish

Q W E R T Y U I O P
A S D F G H J K L
Z X C V B N M

Clue: darkness

EXPERT

Puzzle 176

EXPERT

B E F I T

B R E A D

S A L V O

QWERTYUIOP
ASDFGHJKL
ZXCVBNM

_ _ _ _ _

Clue: spoon

E I G H T

S P A C E

A U D I O

QWERTYUIOP
ASDFGHJKL
ZXCVBNM

_ _ _ _ _

Clue: inundation

B L E A K

V I S T A

A M A S S

QWERTYUIOP
ASDFGHJKL
ZXCVBNM

_ _ _ _ _

Clue: muffler

I D I O T

P U P A L

S A U N A

QWERTYUIOP
ASDFGHJKL
ZXCVBNM

_ _ _ _ _

Clue: signal

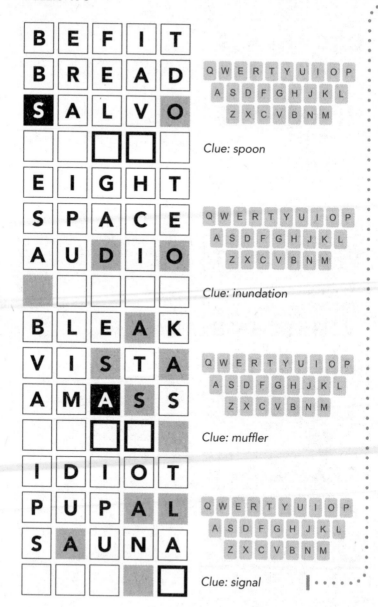

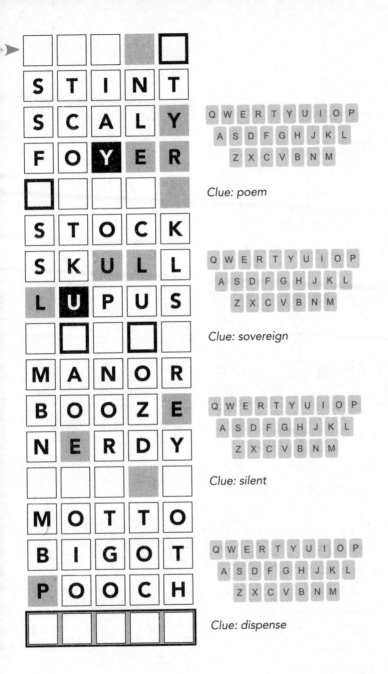

S	T	I	N	T
S	C	A	L	Y
F	O	Y	E	R
S	T	O	C	K
S	K	U	L	L
L	U	P	U	S
M	A	N	O	R
B	O	O	Z	E
N	E	R	D	Y
M	O	T	T	O
B	I	G	O	T
P	O	O	C	H

Q W E R T Y U I O P
A S D F G H J K L
Z X C V B N M

Clue: poem

Q W E R T Y U I O P
A S D F G H J K L
Z X C V B N M

Clue: sovereign

Q W E R T Y U I O P
A S D F G H J K L
Z X C V B N M

Clue: silent

Q W E R T Y U I O P
A S D F G H J K L
Z X C V B N M

Clue: dispense

EXPERT

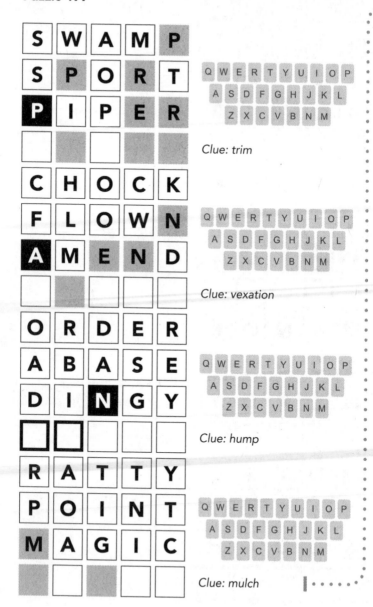

Puzzle 177

S	W	A	M	P
S	P	O	R	T
P	I	P	E	R

Q W E R T Y U I O P
A S D F G H J K L
Z X C V B N M

Clue: trim

C	H	O	C	K
F	L	O	W	N
A	M	E	N	D

Q W E R T Y U I O P
A S D F G H J K L
Z X C V B N M

Clue: vexation

EXPERT

O	R	D	E	R
A	B	A	S	E
D	I	N	G	Y

Q W E R T Y U I O P
A S D F G H J K L
Z X C V B N M

Clue: hump

R	A	T	T	Y
P	O	I	N	T
M	A	G	I	C

Q W E R T Y U I O P
A S D F G H J K L
Z X C V B N M

Clue: mulch

U	D	D	E	R	
S	P	A	S	M	
M	O	U	N	D	
					Clue: stride
L	A	G	E	R	
B	I	O	M	E	
E	N	E	M	Y	
					Clue: dot
D	O	Z	E	N	
G	R	O	O	M	
M	I	T	R	E	
					Clue: rascal
C	I	G	A	R	
S	U	N	N	Y	
C	R	E	E	P	
					Clue: device

Q W E R T Y U I O P
A S D F G H J K L
Z X C V B N M

Puzzle 178

H	E	D	G	E	
L	A	T	H	E	Q W E R T Y U I O P
R	E	V	U	E	A S D F G H J K L Z X C V B N M
					Clue: redbreast
A	U	D	I	O	
B	R	O	A	D	Q W E R T Y U I O P
M	O	T	O	R	A S D F G H J K L Z X C V B N M
					Clue: stirred
C	A	R	R	Y	
P	R	O	U	D	Q W E R T Y U I O P
S	L	I	M	E	A S D F G H J K L Z X C V B N M
					Clue: publication
C	A	V	I	L	
P	O	S	S	E	Q W E R T Y U I O P
R	I	V	E	R	A S D F G H J K L Z X C V B N M
					Clue: bone

EXPERT

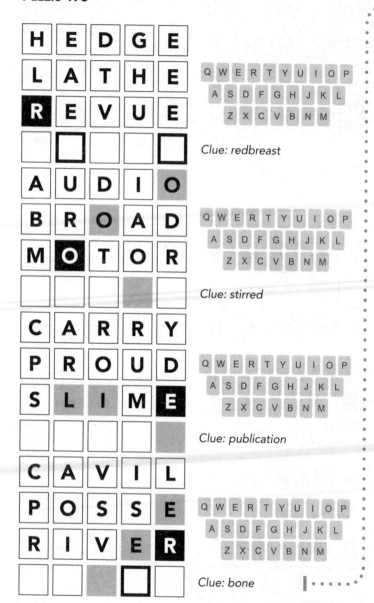

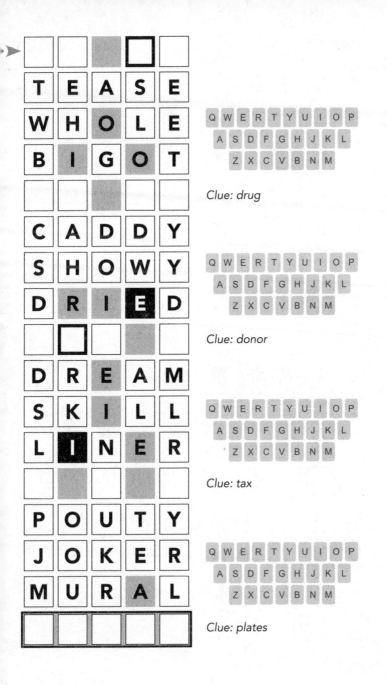

T	E	A	S	E
W	H	O	L	E
B	I	G	O	T
C	A	D	D	Y
S	H	O	W	Y
D	R	I	E	D
D	R	E	A	M
S	K	I	L	L
L	I	N	E	R
P	O	U	T	Y
J	O	K	E	R
M	U	R	A	L

Q W E R T Y U I O P
A S D F G H J K L
Z X C V B N M

Clue: drug

Q W E R T Y U I O P
A S D F G H J K L
Z X C V B N M

Clue: donor

Q W E R T Y U I O P
A S D F G H J K L
Z X C V B N M

Clue: tax

Q W E R T Y U I O P
A S D F G H J K L
Z X C V B N M

Clue: plates

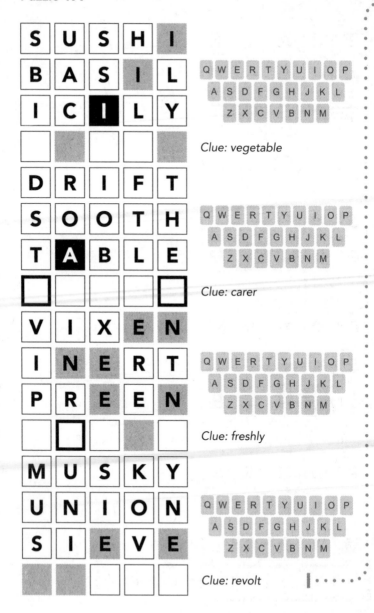

EXPERT

Puzzle 179

S	U	S	H	I
B	A	S	I	L
I	C	I	L	Y

Q W E R T Y U I O P
A S D F G H J K L
Z X C V B N M

Clue: vegetable

D	R	I	F	T
S	O	O	T	H
T	A	B	L	E

Q W E R T Y U I O P
A S D F G H J K L
Z X C V B N M

Clue: carer

V	I	X	E	N
I	N	E	R	T
P	R	E	E	N

Q W E R T Y U I O P
A S D F G H J K L
Z X C V B N M

Clue: freshly

M	U	S	K	Y
U	N	I	O	N
S	I	E	V	E

Q W E R T Y U I O P
A S D F G H J K L
Z X C V B N M

Clue: revolt

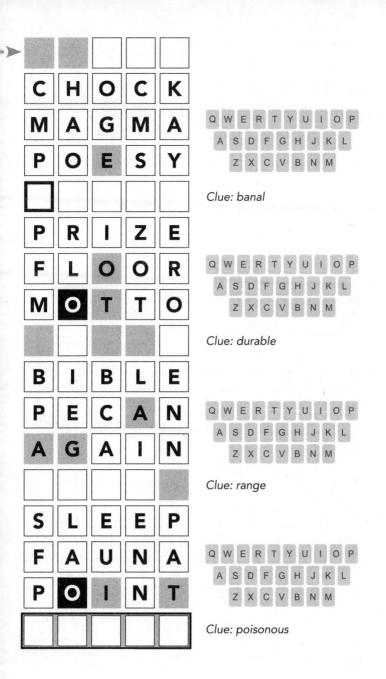

C	H	O	C	K
M	A	G	M	A
P	O	E	S	Y
P	R	I	Z	E
F	L	O	O	R
M	O	T	T	O
B	I	B	L	E
P	E	C	A	N
A	G	A	I	N
S	L	E	E	P
F	A	U	N	A
P	O	I	N	T

Q W E R T Y U I O P
A S D F G H J K L
Z X C V B N M

Clue: banal

Q W E R T Y U I O P
A S D F G H J K L
Z X C V B N M

Clue: durable

Q W E R T Y U I O P
A S D F G H J K L
Z X C V B N M

Clue: range

Q W E R T Y U I O P
A S D F G H J K L
Z X C V B N M

Clue: poisonous

Puzzle 180

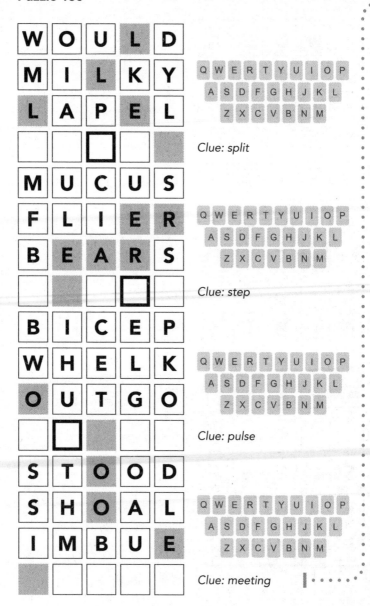

W	O	U	L	D	
M	I	L	K	Y	
L	A	P	E	L	
					Clue: split
M	U	C	U	S	
F	L	I	E	R	
B	E	A	R	S	
					Clue: step
B	I	C	E	P	
W	H	E	L	K	
O	U	T	G	O	
					Clue: pulse
S	T	O	O	D	
S	H	O	A	L	
I	M	B	U	E	
					Clue: meeting

Q W E R T Y U I O P
A S D F G H J K L
Z X C V B N M

Q W E R T Y U I O P
A S D F G H J K L
Z X C V B N M

Q W E R T Y U I O P
A S D F G H J K L
Z X C V B N M

Q W E R T Y U I O P
A S D F G H J K L
Z X C V B N M

B	L	U	N	T	
U	N	I	F	Y	QWERTYUIOP ASDFGHJKL ZXCVBNM
N	I	N	J	A	
					Clue: bitter
D	I	Z	Z	Y	
G	O	D	L	Y	QWERTYUIOP ASDFGHJKL ZXCVBNM
M	O	T	E	L	
					Clue: bird
E	M	P	T	Y	
A	L	O	U	D	QWERTYUIOP ASDFGHJKL ZXCVBNM
A	M	O	N	G	
					Clue: serpent
M	O	T	O	R	
L	O	Y	A	L	QWERTYUIOP ASDFGHJKL ZXCVBNM
P	I	L	O	T	
					Clue: pull

EXPERT

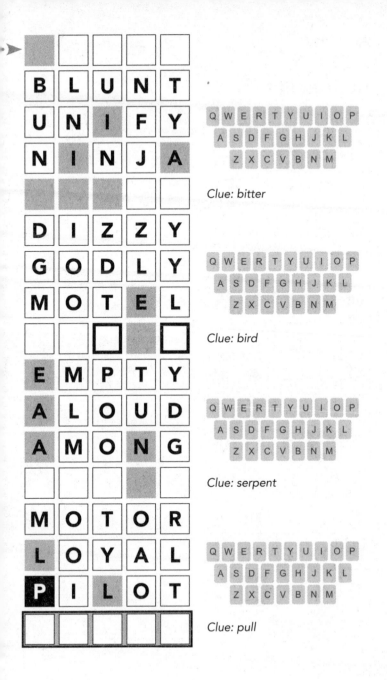

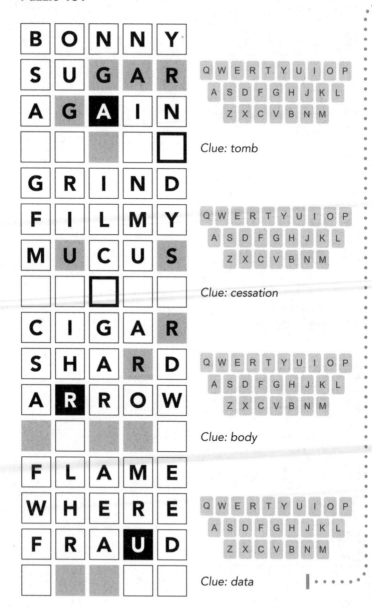

Puzzle 181

B	O	N	N	Y	
S	U	G	A	R	Q W E R T Y U I O P A S D F G H J K L Z X C V B N M
A	G	A	I	N	
					Clue: *tomb*
G	R	I	N	D	
F	I	L	M	Y	Q W E R T Y U I O P A S D F G H J K L Z X C V B N M
M	U	C	U	S	
					Clue: *cessation*
C	I	G	A	R	
S	H	A	R	D	Q W E R T Y U I O P A S D F G H J K L Z X C V B N M
A	R	R	O	W	
					Clue: *body*
F	L	A	M	E	
W	H	E	R	E	Q W E R T Y U I O P A S D F G H J K L Z X C V B N M
F	R	A	U	D	
					Clue: *data*

EXPERT

C	A	R	G	O
I	D	I	O	T
B	O	O	S	T

Q W E R T Y U I O P
A S D F G H J K L
Z X C V B N M

Clue: mobile

B	A	D	L	Y
B	L	A	S	T
L	O	Y	A	L

Q W E R T Y U I O P
A S D F G H J K L
Z X C V B N M

Clue: cloth

B	U	G	G	Y
Z	O	N	A	L
S	A	L	L	Y

Q W E R T Y U I O P
A S D F G H J K L
Z X C V B N M

Clue: enough

O	L	D	E	R
T	H	O	R	N
A	R	R	O	W

Q W E R T Y U I O P
A S D F G H J K L
Z X C V B N M

Clue: scrap

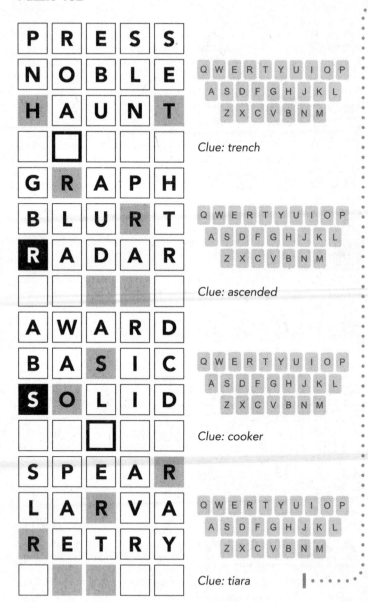

EXPERT

Puzzle 182

P	R	E	S	S
N	O	B	L	E
H	A	U	N	T

QWERTYUIOP
ASDFGHJKL
ZXCVBNM

Clue: trench

G	R	A	P	H
B	L	U	R	T
R	A	D	A	R

QWERTYUIOP
ASDFGHJKL
ZXCVBNM

Clue: ascended

A	W	A	R	D
B	A	S	I	C
S	O	L	I	D

QWERTYUIOP
ASDFGHJKL
ZXCVBNM

Clue: cooker

S	P	E	A	R
L	A	R	V	A
R	E	T	R	Y

QWERTYUIOP
ASDFGHJKL
ZXCVBNM

Clue: tiara

S	T	E	A	M
T	E	A	C	H
M	A	N	G	A
D	E	F	E	R
O	V	E	R	T
R	U	R	A	L
A	L	P	H	A
V	E	N	U	E
S	T	O	K	E
Q	U	O	T	E
B	A	K	E	R
R	E	M	I	T

Q W E R T Y U I O P
A S D F G H J K L
Z X C V B N M

Clue: shaver

Q W E R T Y U I O P
A S D F G H J K L
Z X C V B N M

Clue: hazardous

Q W E R T Y U I O P
A S D F G H J K L
Z X C V B N M

Clue: boat

Q W E R T Y U I O P
A S D F G H J K L
Z X C V B N M

Clue: words

Puzzle 183

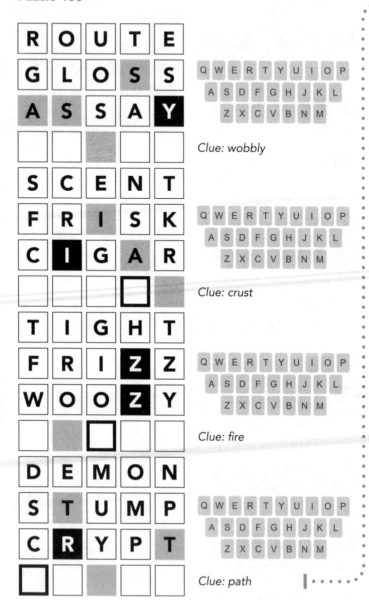

EXPERT

R	O	U	T	E	
G	L	O	S	S	Q W E R T Y U I O P
A	S	S	A	Y	A S D F G H J K L
					Z X C V B N M
					Clue: wobbly
S	C	E	N	T	
F	R	I	S	K	Q W E R T Y U I O P
C	I	G	A	R	A S D F G H J K L
					Z X C V B N M
					Clue: crust
T	I	G	H	T	
F	R	I	Z	Z	Q W E R T Y U I O P
W	O	O	Z	Y	A S D F G H J K L
					Z X C V B N M
					Clue: fire
D	E	M	O	N	
S	T	U	M	P	Q W E R T Y U I O P
C	R	Y	P	T	A S D F G H J K L
					Z X C V B N M
					Clue: path

C	H	A	I	N
N	O	M	A	D
L	A	R	V	A
L	I	M	I	T
G	R	A	C	E
V	I	S	O	R
U	N	D	I	D
J	U	I	C	E
L	U	C	K	Y
S	M	E	A	R
O	P	E	R	A
A	G	A	I	N

Q W E R T Y U I O P
A S D F G H J K L
Z X C V B N M

Clue: delicious

Q W E R T Y U I O P
A S D F G H J K L
Z X C V B N M

Clue: finicky

Q W E R T Y U I O P
A S D F G H J K L
Z X C V B N M

Clue: hover

Q W E R T Y U I O P
A S D F G H J K L
Z X C V B N M

Clue: plain

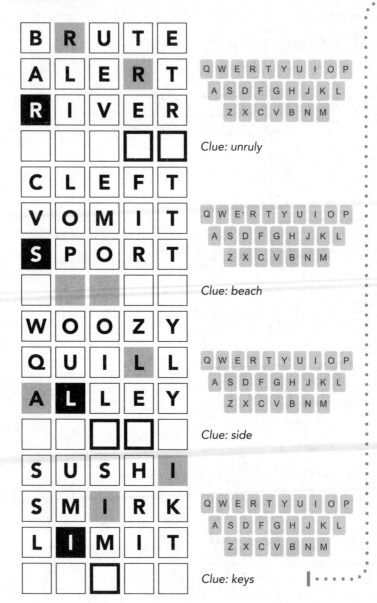

Puzzle 184

B	R	U	T	E
A	L	E	R	T
R	I	V	E	R

Q W E R T Y U I O P
A S D F G H J K L
Z X C V B N M

Clue: unruly

C	L	E	F	T
V	O	M	I	T
S	P	O	R	T

Q W E R T Y U I O P
A S D F G H J K L
Z X C V B N M

Clue: beach

W	O	O	Z	Y
Q	U	I	L	L
A	L	L	E	Y

Q W E R T Y U I O P
A S D F G H J K L
Z X C V B N M

Clue: side

S	U	S	H	I
S	M	I	R	K
L	I	M	I	T

Q W E R T Y U I O P
A S D F G H J K L
Z X C V B N M

Clue: keys

EXPERT

G	O	I	N	G
S	C	O	U	R
F	A	R	C	E

Q W E R T Y U I O P
A S D F G H J K L
Z X C V B N M

Clue: box

M	I	N	I	M
M	A	J	O	R
A	C	U	T	E

Q W E R T Y U I O P
A S D F G H J K L
Z X C V B N M

Clue: parasite

J	U	N	T	A
F	I	N	A	L
A	V	A	I	L

Q W E R T Y U I O P
A S D F G H J K L
Z X C V B N M

Clue: frighten

P	L	U	M	E
A	F	I	R	E
T	R	A	I	T

Q W E R T Y U I O P
A S D F G H J K L
Z X C V B N M

Clue: edges

EXPERT

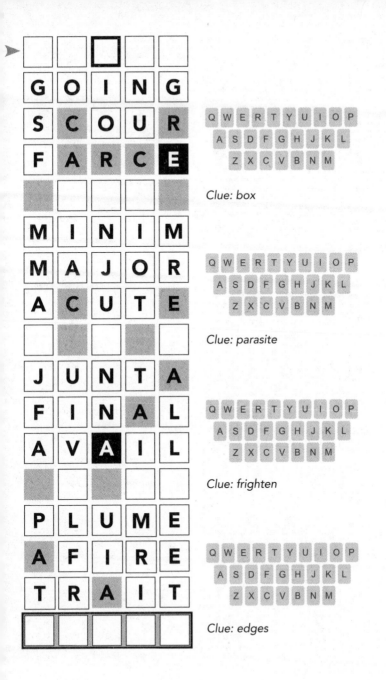

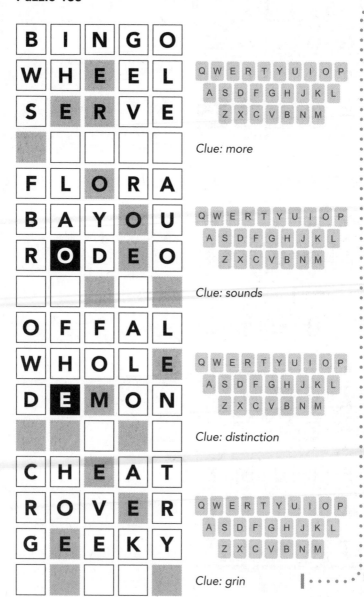

Puzzle 185

B	I	N	G	O
W	H	E	E	L
S	E	R	V	E

QWERTYUIOP
ASDFGHJKL
ZXCVBNM

Clue: more

F	L	O	R	A
B	A	Y	O	U
R	O	D	E	O

QWERTYUIOP
ASDFGHJKL
ZXCVBNM

Clue: sounds

O	F	F	A	L
W	H	O	L	E
D	E	M	O	N

QWERTYUIOP
ASDFGHJKL
ZXCVBNM

Clue: distinction

C	H	E	A	T
R	O	V	E	R
G	E	E	K	Y

QWERTYUIOP
ASDFGHJKL
ZXCVBNM

Clue: grin

EXPERT

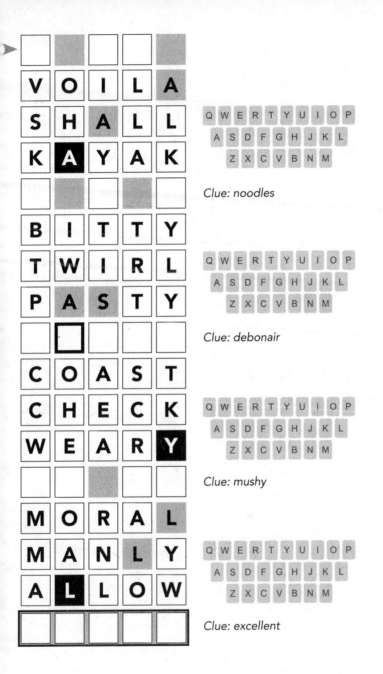

V	O	I	L	A
S	H	A	L	L
K	A	Y	A	K

QWERTYUIOP
ASDFGHJKL
ZXCVBNM

Clue: noodles

B	I	T	T	Y
T	W	I	R	L
P	A	S	T	Y

QWERTYUIOP
ASDFGHJKL
ZXCVBNM

Clue: debonair

C	O	A	S	T
C	H	E	C	K
W	E	A	R	Y

QWERTYUIOP
ASDFGHJKL
ZXCVBNM

Clue: mushy

M	O	R	A	L
M	A	N	L	Y
A	L	L	O	W

QWERTYUIOP
ASDFGHJKL
ZXCVBNM

Clue: excellent

EXPERT

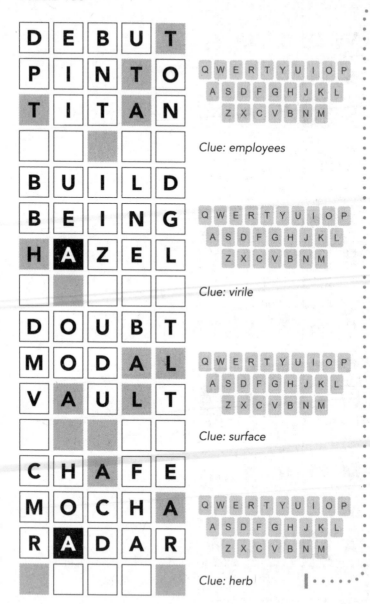

Puzzle 186

EXPERT

D	E	B	U	T
P	I	N	T	O
T	I	T	A	N

Q W E R T Y U I O P
A S D F G H J K L
Z X C V B N M

Clue: employees

B	U	I	L	D
B	E	I	N	G
H	A	Z	E	L

Q W E R T Y U I O P
A S D F G H J K L
Z X C V B N M

Clue: virile

D	O	U	B	T
M	O	D	A	L
V	A	U	L	T

Q W E R T Y U I O P
A S D F G H J K L
Z X C V B N M

Clue: surface

C	H	A	F	E
M	O	C	H	A
R	A	D	A	R

Q W E R T Y U I O P
A S D F G H J K L
Z X C V B N M

Clue: herb

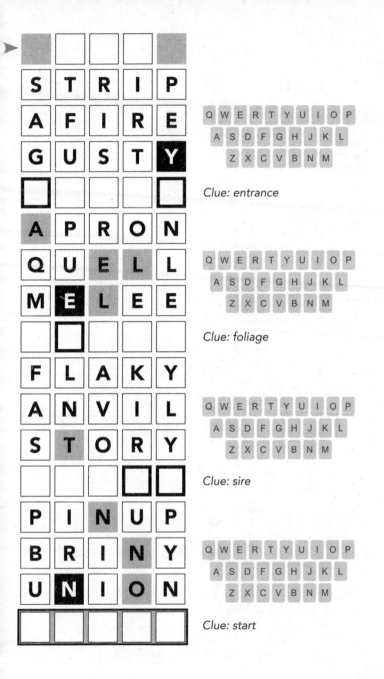

S	T	R	I	P
A	F	I	R	E
G	U	S	T	Y
A	P	R	O	N
Q	U	E	L	L
M	E	L	E	E
F	L	A	K	Y
A	N	V	I	L
S	T	O	R	Y
P	I	N	U	P
B	R	I	N	Y
U	N	I	O	N

Q W E R T Y U I O P
A S D F G H J K L
Z X C V B N M

Clue: entrance

Q W E R T Y U I O P
A S D F G H J K L
Z X C V B N M

Clue: foliage

Q W E R T Y U I O P
A S D F G H J K L
Z X C V B N M

Clue: sire

Q W E R T Y U I O P
A S D F G H J K L
Z X C V B N M

Clue: start

EXPERT

Puzzle 187

D	E	B	I	T
U	N	T	I	E
T	E	S	T	Y
P	R	I	M	E
L	Y	I	N	G
H	A	V	O	C
F	L	I	C	K
G	I	D	D	Y
G	R	A	V	Y
R	E	O	R	G
B	L	U	S	H
B	E	L	L	Y

Q W E R T Y U I O P
A S D F G H J K L
Z X C V B N M

Clue: rubbish

Q W E R T Y U I O P
A S D F G H J K L
Z X C V B N M

Clue: about

Q W E R T Y U I O P
A S D F G H J K L
Z X C V B N M

Clue: singer

Q W E R T Y U I O P
A S D F G H J K L
Z X C V B N M

Clue: machine

EXPERT

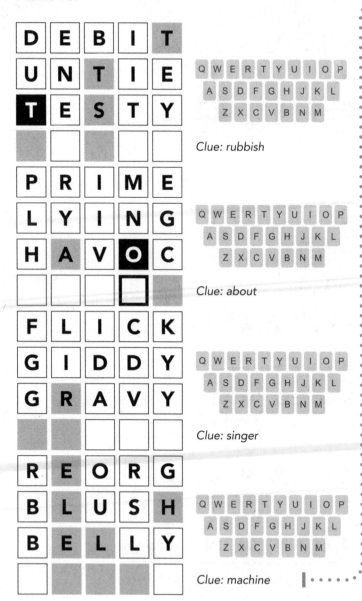

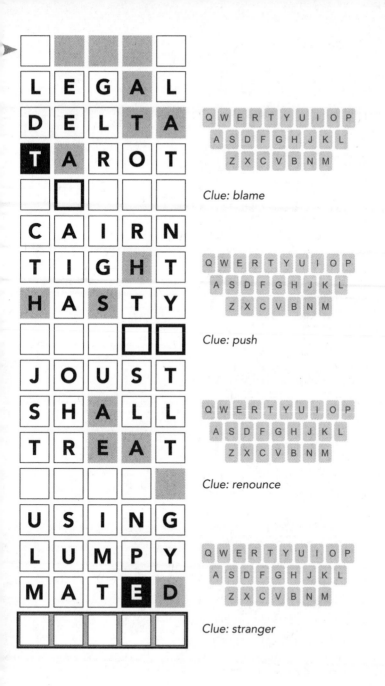

L	E	G	A	L
D	E	L	T	A
T	A	R	O	T
C	A	I	R	N
T	I	G	H	T
H	A	S	T	Y
J	O	U	S	T
S	H	A	L	L
T	R	E	A	T
U	S	I	N	G
L	U	M	P	Y
M	A	T	E	D

Q W E R T Y U I O P
A S D F G H J K L
Z X C V B N M

Clue: blame

Q W E R T Y U I O P
A S D F G H J K L
Z X C V B N M

Clue: push

Q W E R T Y U I O P
A S D F G H J K L
Z X C V B N M

Clue: renounce

Q W E R T Y U I O P
A S D F G H J K L
Z X C V B N M

Clue: stranger

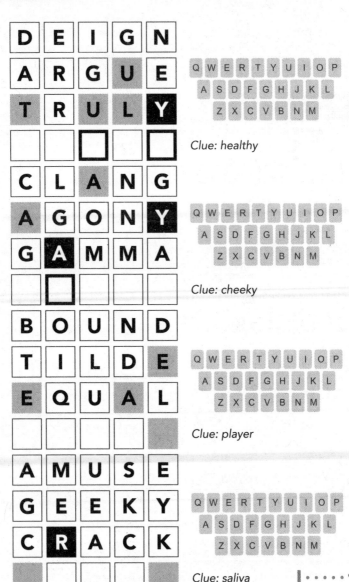

EXPERT

Puzzle 188

D	E	I	G	N	
A	R	G	U	E	Q W E R T Y U I O P A S D F G H J K L Z X C V B N M
T	R	U	L	Y	
					Clue: healthy
C	L	A	N	G	
A	G	O	N	Y	Q W E R T Y U I O P A S D F G H J K L Z X C V B N M
G	A	M	M	A	
					Clue: cheeky
B	O	U	N	D	
T	I	L	D	E	Q W E R T Y U I O P A S D F G H J K L Z X C V B N M
E	Q	U	A	L	
					Clue: player
A	M	U	S	E	
G	E	E	K	Y	Q W E R T Y U I O P A S D F G H J K L Z X C V B N M
C	R	A	C	K	
					Clue: saliva

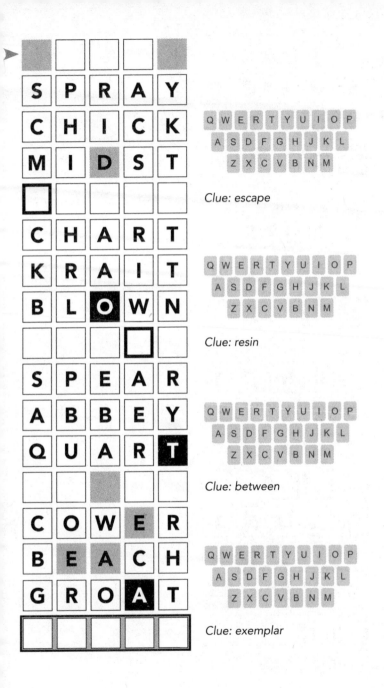

S	P	R	A	Y
C	H	I	C	K
M	I	D	S	T
C	H	A	R	T
K	R	A	I	T
B	L	O	W	N
S	P	E	A	R
A	B	B	E	Y
Q	U	A	R	T
C	O	W	E	R
B	E	A	C	H
G	R	O	A	T

Q W E R T Y U I O P
A S D F G H J K L
Z X C V B N M

Clue: escape

Q W E R T Y U I O P
A S D F G H J K L
Z X C V B N M

Clue: resin

Q W E R T Y U I O P
A S D F G H J K L
Z X C V B N M

Clue: between

Q W E R T Y U I O P
A S D F G H J K L
Z X C V B N M

Clue: exemplar

Puzzle 189

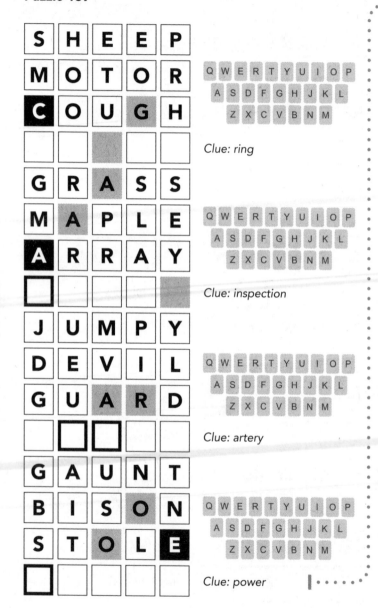

S	H	E	E	P
M	O	T	O	R
C	O	U	G	H
G	R	A	S	S
M	A	P	L	E
A	R	R	A	Y
J	U	M	P	Y
D	E	V	I	L
G	U	A	R	D
G	A	U	N	T
B	I	S	O	N
S	T	O	L	E

Q W E R T Y U I O P
A S D F G H J K L
Z X C V B N M

Clue: ring

Q W E R T Y U I O P
A S D F G H J K L
Z X C V B N M

Clue: inspection

Q W E R T Y U I O P
A S D F G H J K L
Z X C V B N M

Clue: artery

Q W E R T Y U I O P
A S D F G H J K L
Z X C V B N M

Clue: power

EXPERT

A	R	R	O	W	
D	E	M	U	R	Q W E R T Y U I O P A S D F G H J K L Z X C V B N M
U	N	S	E	T	
					Clue: totally
F	I	G	H	T	
C	R	E	S	T	Q W E R T Y U I O P A S D F G H J K L Z X C V B N M
S	H	U	C	K	
					Clue: common
G	R	I	M	E	
F	I	R	S	T	Q W E R T Y U I O P A S D F G H J K L Z X C V B N M
S	P	O	R	E	
					Clue: will
R	E	U	S	E	
N	I	N	T	H	Q W E R T Y U I O P A S D F G H J K L Z X C V B N M
A	S	H	E	N	
					Clue: wintery

EXPERT

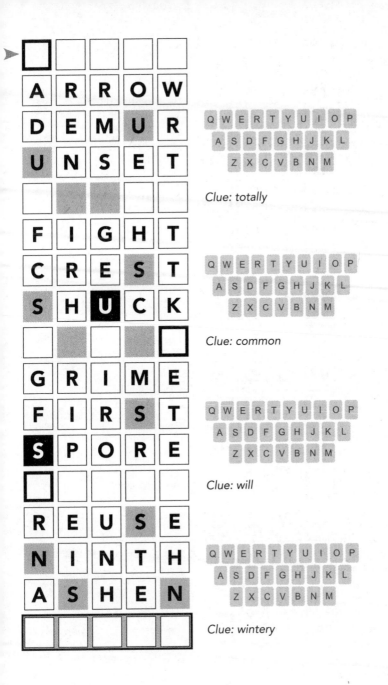

Puzzle 190

S	W	E	A	R
S	P	R	I	G
O	U	T	G	O
T	H	I	N	G
U	S	A	G	E
B	A	L	E	R
S	W	O	O	N
G	R	I	N	S
F	R	E	E	R
W	O	W	E	D
R	U	R	A	L
S	A	L	L	Y

Q W E R T Y U I O P
A S D F G H J K L
Z X C V B N M

Clue: dirty

Q W E R T Y U I O P
A S D F G H J K L
Z X C V B N M

Clue: bright

Q W E R T Y U I O P
A S D F G H J K L
Z X C V B N M

Clue: attribute

Q W E R T Y U I O P
A S D F G H J K L
Z X C V B N M

Clue: tissue

EXPERT

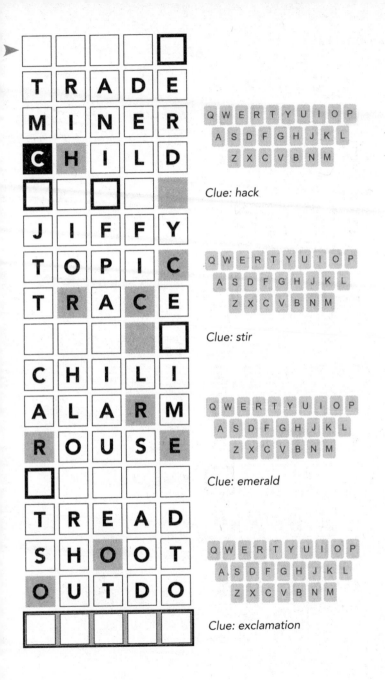

T	R	A	D	E
M	I	N	E	R
C	H	I	L	D
J	I	F	F	Y
T	O	P	I	C
T	R	A	C	E
C	H	I	L	I
A	L	A	R	M
R	O	U	S	E
T	R	E	A	D
S	H	O	O	T
O	U	T	D	O

Q W E R T Y U I O P
A S D F G H J K L
Z X C V B N M

Clue: hack

Q W E R T Y U I O P
A S D F G H J K L
Z X C V B N M

Clue: stir

Q W E R T Y U I O P
A S D F G H J K L
Z X C V B N M

Clue: emerald

Q W E R T Y U I O P
A S D F G H J K L
Z X C V B N M

Clue: exclamation

Puzzle 191

EXPERT

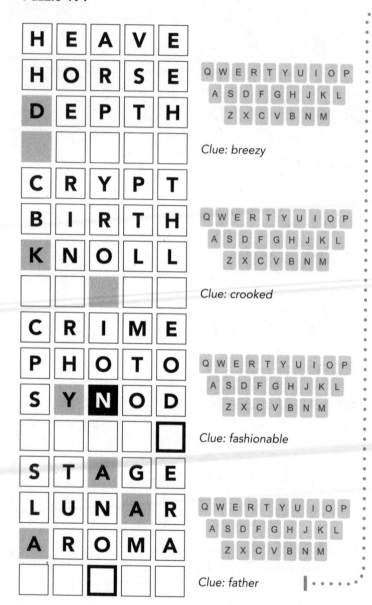

H	E	A	V	E	
H	O	R	S	E	
D	E	P	T	H	
					Clue: *breezy*
C	R	Y	P	T	
B	I	R	T	H	
K	N	O	L	L	
					Clue: *crooked*
C	R	I	M	E	
P	H	O	T	O	
S	Y	N	O	D	
					Clue: *fashionable*
S	T	A	G	E	
L	U	N	A	R	
A	R	O	M	A	
					Clue: *father*

Q W E R T Y U I O P
A S D F G H J K L
Z X C V B N M

Q W E R T Y U I O P
A S D F G H J K L
Z X C V B N M

Q W E R T Y U I O P
A S D F G H J K L
Z X C V B N M

Q W E R T Y U I O P
A S D F G H J K L
Z X C V B N M

H	O	A	R	D
D	I	M	L	Y
P	O	D	G	Y
H	O	O	P	S
F	I	R	S	T
G	L	O	R	Y
D	U	V	E	T
A	M	I	T	Y
M	O	T	T	E
C	H	E	W	S
L	O	V	E	R
C	R	O	W	D

Q W E R T Y U I O P
A S D F G H J K L
Z X C V B N M

Clue: extreme

Q W E R T Y U I O P
A S D F G H J K L
Z X C V B N M

Clue: elegance

Q W E R T Y U I O P
A S D F G H J K L
Z X C V B N M

Clue: strap

Q W E R T Y U I O P
A S D F G H J K L
Z X C V B N M

Clue: populated

EXPERT

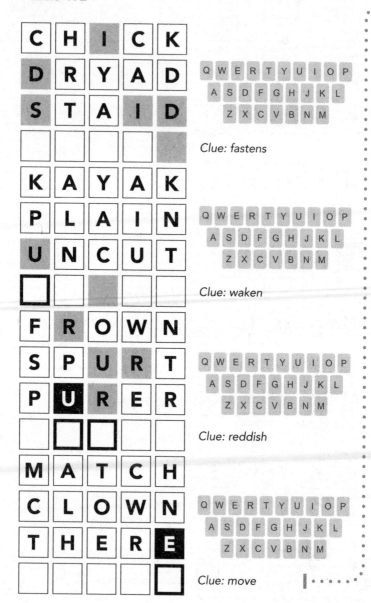

Puzzle 192

C	H	I	C	K
D	R	Y	A	D
S	T	A	I	D
K	A	Y	A	K
P	L	A	I	N
U	N	C	U	T
F	R	O	W	N
S	P	U	R	T
P	U	R	E	R
M	A	T	C	H
C	L	O	W	N
T	H	E	R	E

Q W E R T Y U I O P
A S D F G H J K L
Z X C V B N M

Clue: fastens

Q W E R T Y U I O P
A S D F G H J K L
Z X C V B N M

Clue: waken

Q W E R T Y U I O P
A S D F G H J K L
Z X C V B N M

Clue: reddish

Q W E R T Y U I O P
A S D F G H J K L
Z X C V B N M

Clue: move

EXPERT

D	I	N	G	Y
A	X	I	O	M
T	O	O	T	H
B	L	E	A	K
F	L	U	T	E
D	W	E	L	L
C	L	O	T	H
H	A	N	D	Y
B	R	I	N	E
G	L	O	V	E
W	O	U	N	D
T	H	R	E	W

Q W E R T Y U I O P
A S D F G H J K L
Z X C V B N M

Clue: fumes

Q W E R T Y U I O P
A S D F G H J K L
Z X C V B N M

Clue: happy

Q W E R T Y U I O P
A S D F G H J K L
Z X C V B N M

Clue: bout

Q W E R T Y U I O P
A S D F G H J K L
Z X C V B N M

Clue: stylish

EXPERT

Puzzle 193

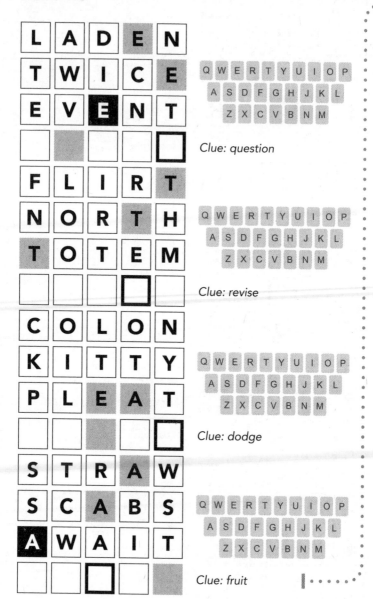

L	A	D	E	N	
T	W	I	C	E	
E	V	E	N	T	
					Clue: question
F	L	I	R	T	
N	O	R	T	H	
T	O	T	E	M	
					Clue: revise
C	O	L	O	N	
K	I	T	T	Y	
P	L	E	A	T	
					Clue: dodge
S	T	R	A	W	
S	C	A	B	S	
A	W	A	I	T	
					Clue: fruit

Q W E R T Y U I O P
A S D F G H J K L
Z X C V B N M

Q W E R T Y U I O P
A S D F G H J K L
Z X C V B N M

Q W E R T Y U I O P
A S D F G H J K L
Z X C V B N M

Q W E R T Y U I O P
A S D F G H J K L
Z X C V B N M

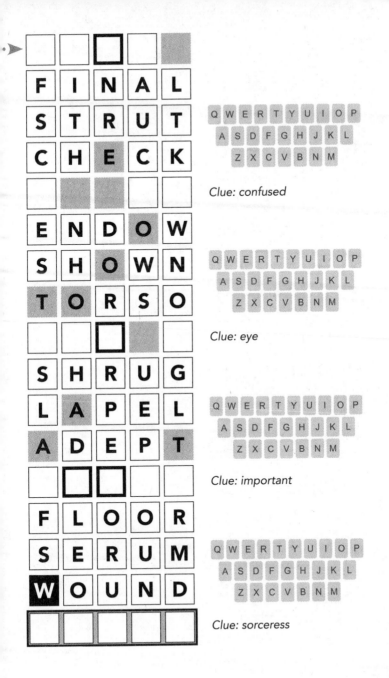

F	I	N	A	L
S	T	R	U	T
C	H	E	C	K
E	N	D	O	W
S	H	O	W	N
T	O	R	S	O
S	H	R	U	G
L	A	P	E	L
A	D	E	P	T
F	L	O	O	R
S	E	R	U	M
W	O	U	N	D

Q W E R T Y U I O P
A S D F G H J K L
Z X C V B N M

Clue: confused

Q W E R T Y U I O P
A S D F G H J K L
Z X C V B N M

Clue: eye

Q W E R T Y U I O P
A S D F G H J K L
Z X C V B N M

Clue: important

Q W E R T Y U I O P
A S D F G H J K L
Z X C V B N M

Clue: sorceress

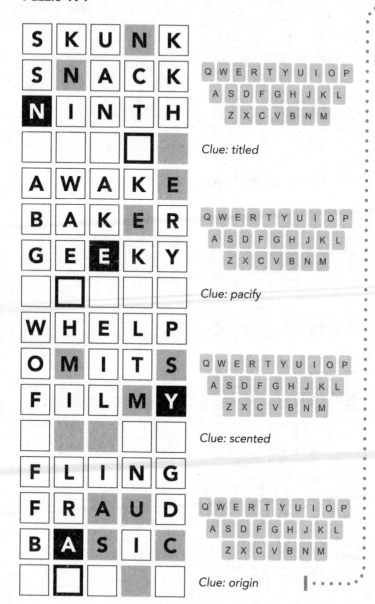

Puzzle 194

S	K	U	N	K
S	N	A	C	K
N	I	N	T	H

Q W E R T Y U I O P
A S D F G H J K L
Z X C V B N M

Clue: titled

A	W	A	K	E
B	A	K	E	R
G	E	E	K	Y

Q W E R T Y U I O P
A S D F G H J K L
Z X C V B N M

Clue: pacify

W	H	E	L	P
O	M	I	T	S
F	I	L	M	Y

Q W E R T Y U I O P
A S D F G H J K L
Z X C V B N M

Clue: scented

F	L	I	N	G
F	R	A	U	D
B	A	S	I	C

Q W E R T Y U I O P
A S D F G H J K L
Z X C V B N M

Clue: origin

EXPERT

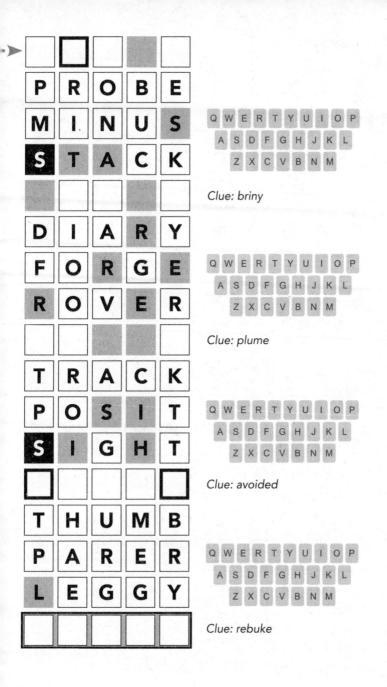

P	R	O	B	E
M	I	N	U	S
S	T	A	C	K
D	I	A	R	Y
F	O	R	G	E
R	O	V	E	R
T	R	A	C	K
P	O	S	I	T
S	I	G	H	T
T	H	U	M	B
P	A	R	E	R
L	E	G	G	Y

Q W E R T Y U I O P
A S D F G H J K L
Z X C V B N M

Clue: briny

Q W E R T Y U I O P
A S D F G H J K L
Z X C V B N M

Clue: plume

Q W E R T Y U I O P
A S D F G H J K L
Z X C V B N M

Clue: avoided

Q W E R T Y U I O P
A S D F G H J K L
Z X C V B N M

Clue: rebuke

EXPERT

Puzzle 195

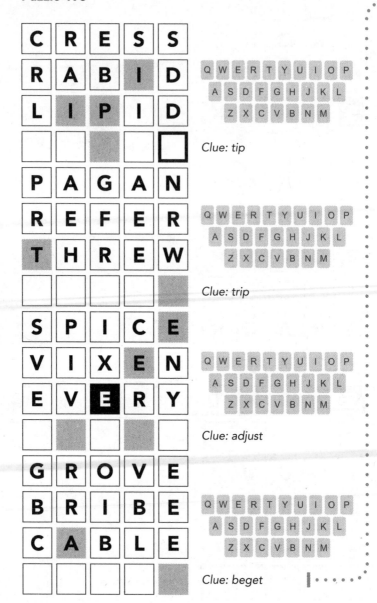

C	R	E	S	S	
R	A	B	I	D	
L	I	P	I	D	
					Clue: *tip*
P	A	G	A	N	
R	E	F	E	R	
T	H	R	E	W	
					Clue: *trip*
S	P	I	C	E	
V	I	X	E	N	
E	V	E	R	Y	
					Clue: *adjust*
G	R	O	V	E	
B	R	I	B	E	
C	A	B	L	E	
					Clue: *beget*

Q W E R T Y U I O P
A S D F G H J K L
Z X C V B N M

Q W E R T Y U I O P
A S D F G H J K L
Z X C V B N M

Q W E R T Y U I O P
A S D F G H J K L
Z X C V B N M

Q W E R T Y U I O P
A S D F G H J K L
Z X C V B N M

EXPERT

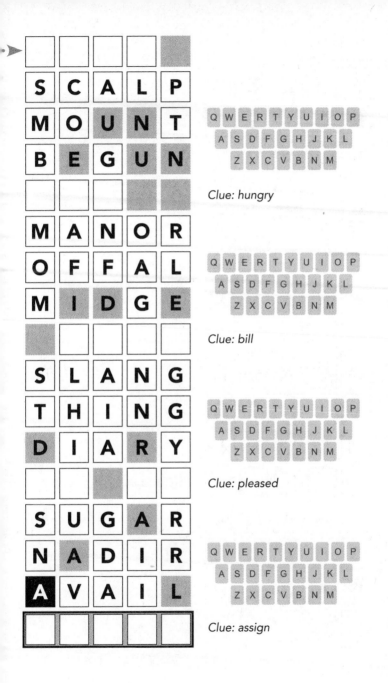

S	C	A	L	P
M	O	U	N	T
B	E	G	U	N

Q W E R T Y U I O P
A S D F G H J K L
Z X C V B N M

Clue: hungry

M	A	N	O	R
O	F	F	A	L
M	I	D	G	E

Q W E R T Y U I O P
A S D F G H J K L
Z X C V B N M

Clue: bill

S	L	A	N	G
T	H	I	N	G
D	I	A	R	Y

Q W E R T Y U I O P
A S D F G H J K L
Z X C V B N M

Clue: pleased

S	U	G	A	R
N	A	D	I	R
A	V	A	I	L

Q W E R T Y U I O P
A S D F G H J K L
Z X C V B N M

Clue: assign

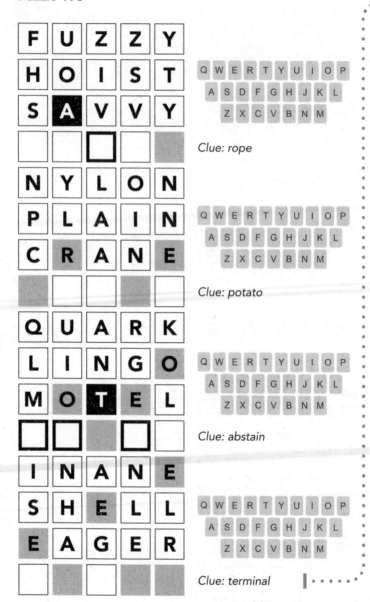

Puzzle 196

F	U	Z	Z	Y	
H	O	I	S	T	QWERTYUIOP
S	A	V	V	Y	ASDFGHJKL ZXCVBNM
					Clue: rope
N	Y	L	O	N	
P	L	A	I	N	QWERTYUIOP
C	R	A	N	E	ASDFGHJKL ZXCVBNM
					Clue: potato
Q	U	A	R	K	
L	I	N	G	O	QWERTYUIOP
M	O	T	E	L	ASDFGHJKL ZXCVBNM
					Clue: abstain
I	N	A	N	E	
S	H	E	L	L	QWERTYUIOP
E	A	G	E	R	ASDFGHJKL ZXCVBNM
					Clue: terminal

EXPERT

H	A	P	P	Y
M	U	C	K	Y
W	O	U	L	D

Q W E R T Y U I O P
A S D F G H J K L
Z X C V B N M

Clue: strength

E	X	A	C	T
P	E	T	A	L
T	E	S	T	Y

Q W E R T Y U I O P
A S D F G H J K L
Z X C V B N M

Clue: tempest

S	M	E	A	R
C	H	A	S	M
C	O	M	M	A

Q W E R T Y U I O P
A S D F G H J K L
Z X C V B N M

Clue: shed

B	O	G	G	Y
E	N	N	U	I
C	U	R	R	Y

Q W E R T Y U I O P
A S D F G H J K L
Z X C V B N M

Clue: larva

EXPERT

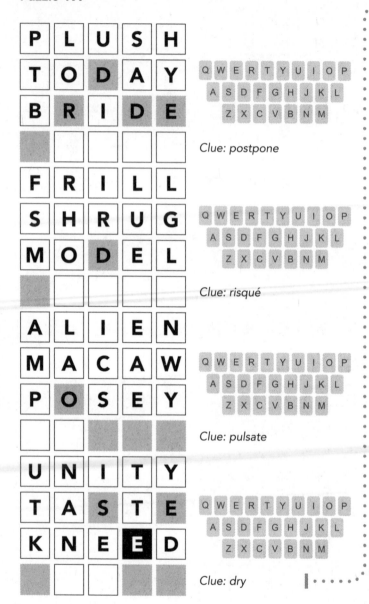

Puzzle 197

P	L	U	S	H
T	O	D	A	Y
B	R	I	D	E

Q W E R T Y U I O P
A S D F G H J K L
Z X C V B N M

Clue: postpone

F	R	I	L	L
S	H	R	U	G
M	O	D	E	L

Q W E R T Y U I O P
A S D F G H J K L
Z X C V B N M

Clue: risqué

A	L	I	E	N
M	A	C	A	W
P	O	S	E	Y

Q W E R T Y U I O P
A S D F G H J K L
Z X C V B N M

Clue: pulsate

U	N	I	T	Y
T	A	S	T	E
K	N	E	E	D

Q W E R T Y U I O P
A S D F G H J K L
Z X C V B N M

Clue: dry

EXPERT

M	A	N	L	Y
D	O	W	N	Y
T	W	E	E	D
G	L	A	D	E
C	R	A	Z	E
H	O	T	E	L
D	I	R	A	M
V	A	L	V	E
R	U	R	A	L
L	I	E	G	E
J	E	R	K	Y
F	O	R	U	M

Q W E R T Y U I O P
A S D F G H J K L
Z X C V B N M

Clue: grab

Q W E R T Y U I O P
A S D F G H J K L
Z X C V B N M

Clue: lichen

Q W E R T Y U I O P
A S D F G H J K L
Z X C V B N M

Clue: revise

Q W E R T Y U I O P
A S D F G H J K L
Z X C V B N M

Clue: seaside

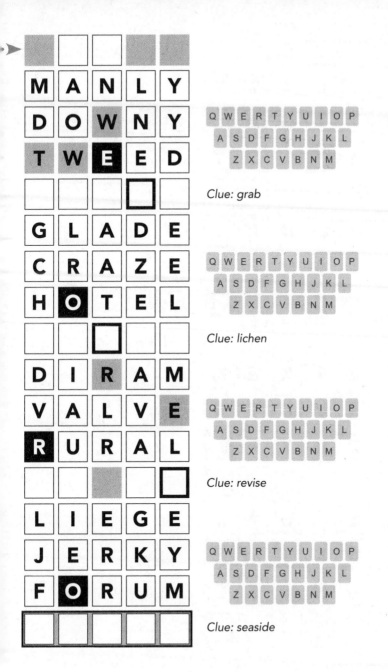

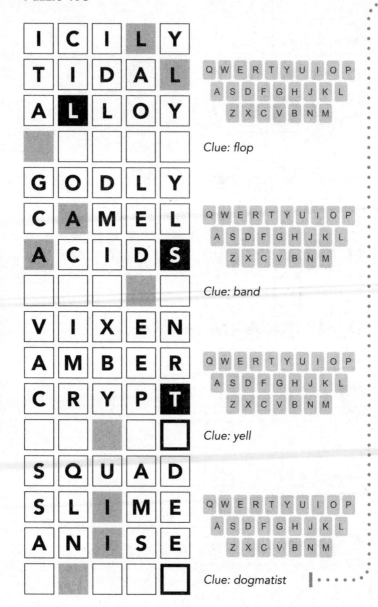

Puzzle 198

I	C	I	L	Y
T	I	D	A	L
A	L	L	O	Y

Q W E R T Y U I O P
A S D F G H J K L
Z X C V B N M

Clue: flop

G	O	D	L	Y
C	A	M	E	L
A	C	I	D	S

Q W E R T Y U I O P
A S D F G H J K L
Z X C V B N M

Clue: band

V	I	X	E	N
A	M	B	E	R
C	R	Y	P	T

Q W E R T Y U I O P
A S D F G H J K L
Z X C V B N M

Clue: yell

S	Q	U	A	D
S	L	I	M	E
A	N	I	S	E

Q W E R T Y U I O P
A S D F G H J K L
Z X C V B N M

Clue: dogmatist

EXPERT

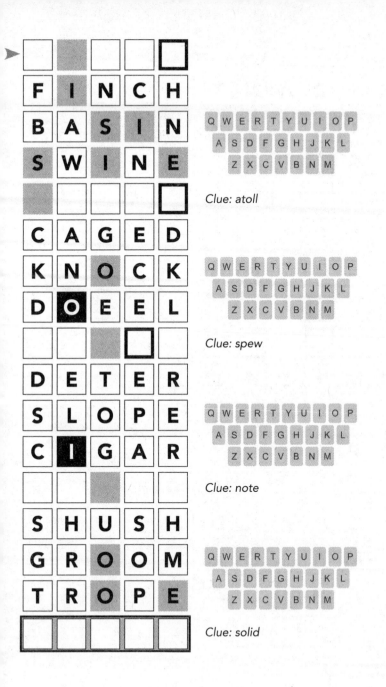

F	I	N	C	H
B	A	S	I	N
S	W	I	N	E
C	A	G	E	D
K	N	O	C	K
D	O	E	E	L
D	E	T	E	R
S	L	O	P	E
C	I	G	A	R
S	H	U	S	H
G	R	O	O	M
T	R	O	P	E

Q W E R T Y U I O P
A S D F G H J K L
Z X C V B N M

Clue: atoll

Q W E R T Y U I O P
A S D F G H J K L
Z X C V B N M

Clue: spew

Q W E R T Y U I O P
A S D F G H J K L
Z X C V B N M

Clue: note

Q W E R T Y U I O P
A S D F G H J K L
Z X C V B N M

Clue: solid

EXPERT

Puzzle 199

P	R	A	N	K
T	O	R	C	H
S	H	O	U	T

Q W E R T Y U I O P
A S D F G H J K L
Z X C V B N M

Clue: during

F	R	A	I	L
A	M	O	N	G
K	N	A	V	E

Q W E R T Y U I O P
A S D F G H J K L
Z X C V B N M

Clue: batchelor

M	I	L	K	Y
F	I	N	A	L
P	I	N	N	Y

Q W E R T Y U I O P
A S D F G H J K L
Z X C V B N M

Clue: subordinate

S	H	A	R	D
M	A	J	O	R
A	R	R	O	W

Q W E R T Y U I O P
A S D F G H J K L
Z X C V B N M

Clue: strapping

EXPERT

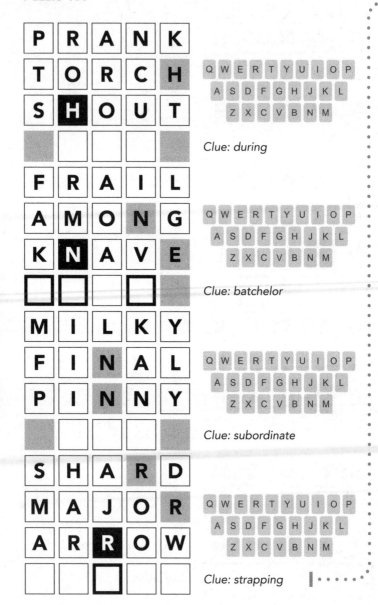

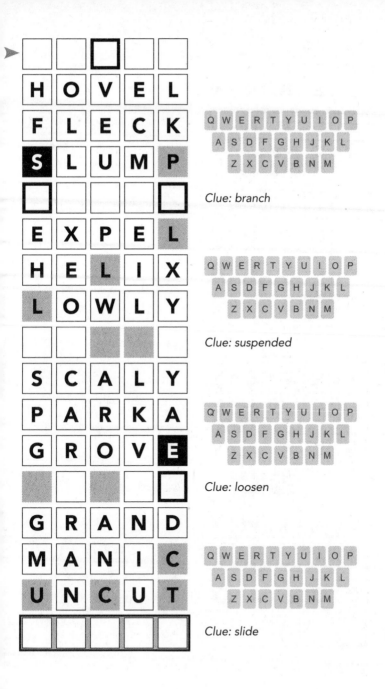

HOVEL
FLECK
SLUMP
EXPEL
HELIX
LOWLY
SCALY
PARKA
GROVE
GRAND
MANIC
UNCUT

Q W E R T Y U I O P
A S D F G H J K L
Z X C V B N M

Clue: branch

Q W E R T Y U I O P
A S D F G H J K L
Z X C V B N M

Clue: suspended

Q W E R T Y U I O P
A S D F G H J K L
Z X C V B N M

Clue: loosen

Q W E R T Y U I O P
A S D F G H J K L
Z X C V B N M

Clue: slide

EXPERT

Puzzle 200

Y	E	A	R	N
A	L	P	H	A
G	O	O	S	E

Q W E R T Y U I O P
A S D F G H J K L
Z X C V B N M

Clue: search

S	H	R	U	G
F	L	O	R	A
P	R	I	O	R

Q W E R T Y U I O P
A S D F G H J K L
Z X C V B N M

Clue: brook

I	N	D	E	X
N	O	O	S	E
E	S	S	A	Y

Q W E R T Y U I O P
A S D F G H J K L
Z X C V B N M

Clue: expand

G	R	I	M	Y
V	A	U	L	T
D	O	L	L	Y

Q W E R T Y U I O P
A S D F G H J K L
Z X C V B N M

Clue: fellow

EXPERT

K	N	E	L	T
C	O	V	E	T
D	A	L	L	Y

Q W E R T Y U I O P
A S D F G H J K L
Z X C V B N M

Clue: assertive

S	C	O	P	E
D	E	T	E	R
T	E	E	T	H

Q W E R T Y U I O P
A S D F G H J K L
Z X C V B N M

Clue: spin

W	A	V	E	R
S	H	A	R	D
G	L	O	V	E

Q W E R T Y U I O P
A S D F G H J K L
Z X C V B N M

Clue: righteously

H	O	V	E	L
G	O	R	G	E
R	E	C	A	P

Q W E R T Y U I O P
A S D F G H J K L
Z X C V B N M

Clue: shape

EXPERT

Solutions

1: SELLS; SMILE; BILLS; **NAILS**
2: CLAIM; VALID; LIVER; **FIELD**
3: BREED; ELDER; RIDES; **HEADS**
4: STEPS; VOTES; HOUSE; **HELLO**
5: QUICK; MUSIC; MINDS; **SIZED**
6: SHARK; SUGAR; BURNS; **SERUM**
7: LIONS; CLIPS; STILL; **HOTEL**
8: CUBIC; CLIMB; BUILT; **SPLIT**
9: PATCH; SPACE; SCOPE; **CORPS**
10: ARROW; MORAL; CREAM; **REALM**
11: ACRES; CURVE; VALUE; **LAUGH**
12: SENDS; ZONES; SOUND; **TURNS**
13: BUCKS; CLUBS; ALBUM; **ADULT**
14: BASIN; BEING; GIANT; **GRAIN**
15: BLOCK; LOOKS; AUTOS; **TURBO**
16: SWEET; SLOPE; LAMPS; **POOLS**
17: FRUIT; FAIRY; RAPID; **PROUD**
18: PLAZA; PANTS; SATIN; **SIGHT**
19: HORSE; HOMES; OTHER; **ACTOR**
20: ALONE; MEANS; NOTES; **DOZEN**
21: DADDY; MEDIA; MILES; **UNITS**
22: ENJOY; NEWLY; UNCLE; **CLONE**
23: MOUSE; LOTUS; SLOTS; **SPELL**
24: HIRED; DRIED; CITED; **CRIME**
25: READS; FARES; NURSE; **DRESS**
26: DIRTY; RIDER; REMIX; **MERIT**
27: SCUBA; USUAL; AWFUL; **FRAUD**
28: CROWD; WOUND; BONDS; **BLOOD**
29: MAKES; JEANS; PHASE; **SHOPS**
30: YOURS; GROSS; SMOKE; **LOCKS**
31: WROTE; ERROR; SORRY; **ROADS**
32: CROPS; POSTS; SPOTS; **TIRES**
33: BIRDS; DROPS; SWORD; **WIRED**
34: LIVES; ALIAS; SALAD; **SANDY**
35: APPLY; TAPES; UPSET; **SPARE**
36: BREAD; BADGE; TRADE; **SEATS**
37: ALLOW; ALONG; ANGLE; **EARLY**
38: VALVE; GRAVE; DREAM; **METAL**
39: TEAMS; SHAME; MAPLE; **MEALS**
40: GROUP; OCCUR; SCORE; **ROUTE**
41: SERVE; RESET; TALES; **TRIAL**
42: DECOR; DROVE; ORDER; **HOPED**
43: FIRES; SAFER; LARGE; **VIRAL**
44: CAKES; CLEAN; PLANT; **PARTY**
45: ACIDS; SCARY; YEARS; **RELAY**
46: SPEED; PANEL; APRIL; **RADIO**
47: CYBER; LYRIC; CAROL; **CHOIR**
48: STORY; PLOTS; DOLLS; **LODGE**
49: FANCY; CRAZY; CARRY; **HEARD**
50: NYLON; LYING; LOGIN; **DOING**
51: PRIME; TERMS; MEETS; **TUNES**
52: QUEST; TUBES; DEMUR; **DODGE**
53: NOBLE; CLOSE; CODES; **OWNED**
54: STOCK; GHOST; MATES; **EARTH**
55: FORCE; CARGO; MACRO; **BOARD**
56: TELLS; LIKES; BIBLE; **BUILD**
57: SCALE; CALLS; SALON; **PLAIN**
58: PIZZA; PAIRS; SHARP; **TRASH**
59: HANDY; DELAY; SALES; **SMELL**
60: WAGON; GAINS; AMONG; **ANIME**
61: WORTH; TOWER; THROW; **NORTH**
62: MIXER; MERCY; ENEMY; **YIELD**
63: CELLS; FALSE; FEELS; **STEEL**
64: CLERK; CORAL; SOLAR; **WALKS**
65: TYPES; DEPTH; DATES; **SEEDS**
66: KARMA; RACKS; CHAOS; **SHOCK**
67: VAULT; VITAL; TILES; **TRAIL**
68: PARKS; SPOKE; EBOOK; **BELOW**
69: VIDEO; NOTED; NEEDS; **GREEN**
70: INBOX; ROBIN; GROWN; **GOING**
71: YARDS; BRASS; SPARE; **PURSE**
72: LADEN; DRAWN; DONOR; **UNION**
73: ADDED; INDEX; KNIFE; **THINK**
74: THICK; TIGHT; CHEST; **TREES**
75: BLANK; BADLY; VALID; **DRAIN**
76: ERROR; DOORS; STORY; **ROLES**
77: BOXED; BEING; GUESS; **TRIES**
78: FIRED; DRAFT; BAKED; **HEARD**
79: POUND; ABODE; DEALT; **FEEDS**
80: SCREW; DRESS; TEXAS; **STRAP**
81: CLOTH; PILOT; COMIC; **CLIFF**
82: NOTES; TOKEN; BROKE; **SEEKS**
83: PRIZE; HORSE; TRUST; **BURST**
84: SHIRT; FLASH; FAILS; **OASIS**
85: DRILL; ALERT; ATLAS; **STAKE**
86: OCEAN; BONES; PROBE; **OXIDE**
87: SEEKS; SCENE; LINKS; **STICK**
88: FUNKY; HUMAN; MANGA; **LOCAL**
89: THREE; CRAFT; EXACT; **AREAS**
90: DODGE; TONER; TRUNK; **QUILT**
91: GAMES; HOUSE; BASED; **MINDS**
92: BATCH; CREAM; POWER; **BRIDE**
93: POKER; GROSS; STORM; **GATES**
94: RISKS; DAIRY; MERIT; **TRACE**
95: FORGE; AFTER; APART; **STEPS**
96: ACUTE; PANIC; MEANS; **FACES**
97: PRESS; PAGES; UPSET; **NEEDS**
98: FROST; MODES; OLDER; **EAGLE**
99: PAIRS; TRIAL; UNTIL; **TILES**
100: NAMED; ROMAN; BRAND; **IDEAL**
101: BADGE; FILED; DAILY; **CLEAN**
102: MALES; SPELL; CLIPS; **PEACE**
103: FRUIT; MIXER; SUITE; **TIGER**
104: THINK; SKIRT; STUFF; **TANKS**
105: ALIAS; POLAR; PROVE; **SHARP**
106: TRICK; SCOUT; TRUCK; **FOCUS**
107: LIMIT; CLIMB; BRING; **GROWN**
108: ISSUE; QUITE; SOUTH; **COINS**
109: CHASE; TRASH; PLAYS; **MEDAL**
110: STYLE; YEARS; READY; **YARDS**
111: REALM; GIRLS; SOLVE; **STORE**
112: WORKS; STUCK; SIXTH; **NIGHT**
113: SHAPE; APPLY; DELAY; **FALLS**
114: KINGS; CHAIN; FAIRY; **MAYBE**
115: ANGER; JEANS; SQUAD; **FACTS**
116: TRIED; DRAIN; AHEAD; **TRADE**
117: PRIDE; SHIPS; HOPED; **SHELL**
118: BUILD; VINYL; PLAIN; **BEGAN**
119: PARTY; CREST; SMART; **MAJOR**
120: DEATH; GAUGE; GUIDE; **EQUAL**
121: START; TALES; EVENT; **TONES**
122: PUMPS; GROUP; USING; **GOODS**
123: BANDS; URBAN; GRAIN; **HANDS**
124: HERBS; PHONE; SHOWN; **FLUSH**
125: WINGS; TIGHT; POINT; **TRAIN**
126: OWNED; WORLD; ALONG; **ANGEL**

127: BLAME; WAGES; BELOW; **PLATE**
128: ARRAY; CARRY; HOURS; **RIGHT**
129: DREAM; FORMS; MORAL; **MAYOR**
130: GHOST; YOURS; RULED; **AMEND**
131: CHILD; DISCS; PICKS; **PRICE**
132: ORBIT; WORRY; LOWER; **WIRED**
133: CASES; DEALT; YACHT; **MARSH**
134: GROVE; VOICE; VIEWS; **SUPER**
135: SHALL; PHASE; RATES; **CACHE**
136: CITED; SWEET; WEIRD; **INNER**
137: STAYS; TAPES; FLAME; **ARMED**
138: SITES; CHESS; SHAME; **ALBUM**
139: MAKER; SMOKE; CAUSE; **SIGMA**
140: FIRST; PARTS; BEAST; **SPIES**
141: MASON; POEMS; SPOKE; **LOOSE**
142: FLOOR; WORSE; WIVES; **GRAVE**
143: HEADS; STATE; PAPER; **HELPS**
144: AMBER; BREED; FRAME; **RADAR**
145: PEARL; LAKES; CHECK; **KNIFE**
146: RIDER; ENTER; FEARS; **FILES**
147: SURGE; ROGER; RULES; **BUILT**
148: DATED; DOUBT; BLOOM; **ROBOT**
149: FLESH; FOCAL; SCOOP; **BACON**
150: MOUNT; SPORT; LATER; **WRITE**
151: HATCH; NYMPH; MAXIM; BLARE; GRIEF; PANIC; SNAKY; **NUTTY**
152: ALTER; ANNUL; APTLY; SPENT; SOBER; CAROL; BENCH; **AUNTY**
153: WORST; STOOD; GUSTY; CRYPT; POLAR; CAPER; BANAL; **APHID**
154: RIVET; VEGAN; GLAND; STEAD; CLASP; ABORT; NOSEY; **UNCLE**
155: CLOUT; ROWER; CHAIR; STAIN; SCRAP; AUGUR; MARSH; **SLINK**
156: FLAKY; PAYEE; COYLY; CHANT; JOINT; PRONE; WAGON; **SWINE**
157: ABODE; THREE; HURRY; DEBAR; PENAL; IRONY; OWNER; **AROSE**
158: SHYLY; SHAFT; BEEFY; FINER; MANGO; ASSET; SATIN; **MOTIF**
159: UNZIP; BLIMP; SOAPY; LOOPY; SPOON; ADAPT; PUREE; **TENTH**
160: VIDEO; DROVE; BLUES; EKING; BADGE; PESKY; SPOOK; **PIQUE**
161: BROOM; OCCUR; TACKY; COBRA; VILLA; GHOUL; FLUNK; **POLKA**
162: PLUMP; CHIRP; THIGH; BONGO; FENCE; RECUR; SCOWL; **ALIEN**
163: SCREW; TAKER; FANCY; BLACK; SULLY; FILTH; SPILT; **TIGER**
164: LOGIN; ALIKE; GUESS; ROGUE; BUTCH; BANJO; RADIO; **AWARE**
165: PLAZA; GLYPH; PINCH; DIODE; FILER; CRUDE; PUPPY; **MORPH**
166: SPINY; CYBER; FEVER; PERIL; HABIT; METRO; FROTH; **BUYER**
167: FOLIO; IGLOO; ATTIC; EJECT; BELIE; AMPLY; BLUER; **ALIBI**
168: SLASH; ACORN; PRAWN; POPPY; CREPT; CHORE; ERODE; **DYING**
169: SWORE; WORLD; GOODS; BEGIN; BESET; SLEPT; HASTE; **MUSHY**
170: ARGUE; SLIDE; WISPY; BELLY; BRAIN; HEAVE; RIVAL; **SHELL**
171: SHOCK; CUMIN; LIPID; AISLE; BUILD; STUFF; WRUNG; **TWICE**
172: MIGHT; QUITE; PATIO; KNEAD; MAYBE; BERTH; BLOOM; **COMFY**
173: DINER; BATON; TABOO; BROOK; BRAID; LABEL; INBOX; **ENVOY**
174: STIFF; STUCK; DOUGH; LATCH; SHORN; SNIPE; WINCE; **COACH**
175: KIOSK; DOWDY; EBONY; HOUSE; GUILD; FUDGE; SNUFF; **NIGHT**
176: SCOOP; FLOOD; SCARF; FLARE; RHYME; RULER; QUIET; **SPEND**
177: PRUNE; ANGER; HUNCH; HUMUS; MARCH; SPECK; SCAMP; **MODEM**
178: ROBIN; WOKEN; TITLE; FEMUR; OPIUM; GIVER; TITHE; **CHINA**
179: ONION; NANNY; NEWLY; REPEL; TRITE; TOUGH; GAMUT; **TOXIC**
180: CLEFT; TREAD; SONAR; COVEN; ACRID; CRANE; SNAKE; **PLUCK**
181: GRAVE; PAUSE; TRUNK; INPUT; PHONE; LINEN; AMPLE; **CRUMB**
182: DITCH; RISEN; STOVE; CROWN; RAZOR; RISKY; SKIFF; **LYRIC**
183: SHAKY; PIZZA; BLAZE; TRAIL; TASTY; FUSSY; FLOAT; **BLAND**
184: ROWDY; SANDY; FLANK; PIANO; CRATE; LEECH; SCARE; **BANKS**
185: EXTRA; NOISE; MERIT; SMILE; RAMEN; SUAVE; PULPY; **ELITE**
186: STAFF; MACHO; PLANE; BASIL; LOBBY; LEAFY; BEGET; **ONSET**
187: TRASH; AFOOT; TENOR; LATHE; THANK; SHOVE; WAIVE; **ODDER**
188: LUSTY; SASSY; GAMER; DROOL; ELUDE; EPOXY; TWIXT; **IDEAL**
189: CLANG; AUDIT; AORTA; FORCE; FULLY; USUAL; SHALL; **SNOWY**
190: MUDDY; JAZZY; BLAME; FLESH; COUGH; CHURN; GREEN; **GOLLY**
191: WINDY; ASKEW; FUNKY; DADDY; UNDUE; GRACE; THONG; **URBAN**
192: BINDS; ROUSE; RUDDY; BUDGE; SMOKE; MERRY; SPREE; **SMART**
193: QUERY; STUDY; EVADE; APPLE; DOPEY; OPTIC; TITAN; **WITCH**
194: NOBLE; QUELL; MUSKY; CAUSE; SALTY; CREST; SHIED; **SCOLD**
195: POINT; VISIT; TWEAK; SPAWN; UNFED; DEBIT; PROUD; **ALLOT**
196: CABLE; TUBER; DETOX; DEPOT; FORTE; STORM; MOULT; **PUPAL**
197: DEFER; BAWDY; THROB; SOBER; WREST; MOSSY; RESET; **COAST**
198: SLUMP; BRASS; SHOUT; BIGOT; ISLET; VOMIT; MINIM; **OAKEN**
199: WHILE; UNWED; UNDER; BURLY; SPRIG; SLUNG; UNTIE; **CHUTE**
200: SCOUT; CREEK; SWELL; BLOKE; BRASH; TWIRL; NOBLY; **CUBIC**

Quarto

First published in 2024 by Ivy Press,
an imprint of The Quarto Group.
One Triptych Place, London
SE1 9SH, United Kingdom
T (0)20 7700 6700

www.Quarto.com

A catalogue record for this book is available from the British Library.

ISBN 978-0-7112-8275-9

10 9 8 7 6 5 4 3 2 1

Devised by Michael Brunström

Compiled and designed by Tim Dedopulos and Roland Hall

Printed and bound by CPI Group (UK) Ltd, Croydon, CR0 4YY

FSC
www.fsc.org
MIX
Paper from responsible sources
FSC® C005010